PICKING UP
THE PIECES

A Collaboration: Stories from Tragedy to Triumph to Faith & Freedom

Rochinda Pickens

Purpose Publishing
1503 Main Street #168 ✖ Grandview, Missouri
www.purposepublishing.com

Copyright © 2017 Rochinda Pickens

ISBN: 978-0-9997999-2-5

Editing by Felicia Murrell
Book Cover Design by PP Designers

All scripture contained in this book are referenced from the New King James Version, The Message, New Living Translation, Amplified and New International Versions of the Bible.

Printed in the United States of America.

Dedication

To women and men around the
world who have decided to
Pick Up The Pieces
and start over!

Acknowledgements

All the Glory and praise to my Heavenly Father God who has been my source from the beginning and will be until the end of time. To my husband, Alan, whom I love and adore with all my heart. Your support in everything I do is appreciated and needed. My children; Brittany, Darrell and Andrea. Your encouragement to do "ME" without holding back is awesome. I love you for the never ending fuel.

I want to personally thank each collaborating author for sharing your truth without hesitation. Together, we will enjoy the process of seeing our "Masterpiece" come to fruition. Thank you for going on this ride with me.

Purpose Publishing, thank you for publishing my second book and making the process smooth.

Table of Contents

Preface

It is time to start Picking up the Pieces and get moving. You have already wasted enough time procrastinating on what your next move will be or have consulted with too many people already about your situation; trying to get everyone's approval. You know and I know what's happening; I've been there and done that. A lot of wasted time and energy. I'm glad you are reading this book. It shows that you are curious about how others have gotten it done. It's okay to be curious. But what you really need is active participation in Picking up the Pieces in your life.

Our stories are here to help you on the journey, oh yes, it is a journey. A "Lifestyle" journey to a different mindset; the mindset of "Freedom." This is not a book of motivational speeches or affirmations. This is a book of real people, with real stories of truths that have changed their lives. Is this a dream or is this the real deal? It's not a dream. It is absolutely the real deal! The Real Deal is that each of us have experienced God's divine intervention. We are representatives; fragments that needed an intervention to save each of our lives! It doesn't matter who you are or what you have been through. In order to begin *Picking up the Pieces*, you must start from the beginning. Each author shares their personal fragment of their broken glass and how they had to piece it together to display their own masterpiece healing.

Chapter 1

Beyond Fear Lies Freedom

The darkness that I once loved so much portrayed itself as light. I felt snuggly and warm in there, and most thought I was quite content. But now that I am truly awake, the freshness from the breeze of anointed air intensifies the space I once hid in. The presence of God has awakened my soul to where I expect only great things in the life that is before me. The darkness was a mixture of abandonment, death, deceit, depression, divorce, doubt, friendship, guilt, and health buried in a solid tomb of no return.

The anxiety of someone finding out I was once lost no longer existed. Would my friends be understanding of my truth or would they stay stuck on the past that had been revealed to the world, wondering if my truth had implicated them in any way of their truth?

When God asks you to move and you resist, he will come back and demand you go, with no further notice. A notice that may come in the wee hour of the night, during your lunch break, while you're shopping or during a terrible ice storm. However God sequesters

you, just be ready. Ready to go into the battlefield of being healed.

To go into the battlefield, you must be equipped with God's covering. A covering that fits eloquently around your entire body. This covering has been mass produced for many body styles, but individually designed just for you. The covering I received started at the beginning of my blonde locs and draped down past my shoulder blades. It was one continuous flow of graceful and loving movement that covered my tall body frame. Although I had God's covering upon me, I didn't recognize it until years later.

God had initiated countless encounters with me over the years, but I ignored all the nudges and the signs that were given. When I say ignored the signs, I'm saying God wasn't given the recognition of all that He had done for me.

"In the beginning God created the heavens and the earth. (Genesis 1). Who do you know that can keep you safe during times of desperation? Who can provide food and shelter when you know your bank account ledger is reading zero and you have fallen behind on your mortgage? What about when you birth children when your body revealed infertility?

The odds have been stacked against me on several occasions. God forgave me and blessed me beyond measure to have the desires of my heart with some added perks. Yes, perks, that's exactly what I call them. The past few years have been mind-blowing, watching my new life unfold before me seamlessly.

I decided to take that first step in 2009, to answer the call of acknowledging my brokenness. Again, I fell short and allowed life to intervene and consume my being. But now, I'm desperate once again and need help and some much-needed answers. Answers that only God can provide.

Get rid of this crutch and make a lifestyle change with the Lord.

Why do we wait for a crisis to take place before we talk to our Heavenly Father? I'm just saying. Shame on us. Yes, you and me! Why didn't I recognize the daunting behavior of brokenness that was still lurking on the inside? I had a "just in case crutch" sitting in the corner waiting to be used.

How many of you all have that same ole

crutch? That crutch was sabotaging my excel into greatness, a greatness that couldn't come out and stand tall amongst my peers. I need you to recognize "the just in case crutch" so you can make the decision to discard, demolish, destroy, and release it today. Yes, right now. Get rid of this crutch and make a lifestyle change with the Lord. I'm saying lifestyle because this is the only way you can experience all that God has for you. If you are reading this book, then you have already decided to pick up the pieces and move forward. Be intentional about your lifestyle with God.

I have picked up the pieces several times in my life and had to start over. Was it easy? Not always, but I had to move forward. You may be wondering how many times it actually took before "Clarity" came?

The clear picture of moving forward came once I surrendered everything else over to God. I remember the last few times I had to pick up the pieces and start over. In the end, it was very captivating.

When you think of captivating, what comes to your mind? Captivating; capable of attracting and holding interest; charming. Captivating for me was allowing myself to be held captive by God's being. Being held captive by God is a safe place for me. A place where protection is always available, and there is no judgment. A very charming and quaint place where I love being kept.

I once surveyed a group of people and asked, "what comes to mind when you hear the phrase picking up the pieces?" The majority said picking up the pieces was a reminder of a dark place that was very painful and a reminder of starting over. I agreed with each response, but I do not agree that picking up the pieces has to be fearful or painful.

You can be fearful of starting over, but you owe it to yourself to start over without allowing fear to interfere in your new beginning. We must give ourselves permission to start over and trust the process. Although the pain and discomfort are unsettling, there is light at the end of the tunnel. Maybe you are not in a tunnel, perhaps you are in a box or a cage, or maybe you are just sitting on the sideline watching and wishing. If you have not begun to pick up the pieces and move forward, then you are stuck in a common place of bondage. An uncomfortable place that is completely filled with discontentment.

Picking up the pieces isn't always because of an unforeseen situation. It could be something that has been sought after and carefully planned out. Many times, we are not prepared to start over or even think about moving forward because of our own doubts and being set in our ways.

Let's assume the start of this season caught you by surprise and you are struggling with how to move forward and pick up the pieces. If you recall the first thing I mentioned was the last time I picked up the pieces was rather captivating. Why? Because I am now in a different place in life and starting over is no longer scary for me. Picking up the pieces became normal for me. The scripture, "Behold, I am doing a new thing; now it springs forth, do you not perceive it? I will make a way in the wilderness and rivers in the desert" (Isaiah 43:19), stays with me through it all. For me, the scripture means whenever I start over in the wilderness, it will be a new thing, but God will make a way. Define your own "NEW."

The question for many will be how do you start over and where do you begin? You first must decide to take the first step, leap, or jump. Some of us may have to just pack up our cars and trucks or rent a U-Haul and hit the highway. Whatever that first step looks like for you, let's make sure we are clear on what's happening and map out the first few months of direction for where we are headed. Maybe you don't know where you are headed, but you know you must start somewhere.

First, you want to make sure your quest is the Divine Instruction of God. What have you been praying for? If you haven't been in conversation with God and your prayer life has fallen off, I suggest you go back to that space. If you remember in my first book, "From Being Kept to Being Kept", the first chapter was How Do I Begin? That chapter still remains true for me. We start from the beginning. When we try to pick up the pieces from the middle or the end, we never totally put everything together. Imagine trying to bake your favorite dessert and starting from the bottom of the recipe. That would be a total disaster. Picking up the pieces is your very own award-winning recipe.

> *Most of the time we are not operating in our own truth, therefore the lies we have told society stagnate our walk.*

As you navigate your way with your award-winning recipe, how does it feel? Let me share with you how I used to feel. My mind always felt cluttered with those 'what if' questions. Let's call them *self-doubt*. My stomach was always knotted up and upset. That would be called nervousness. I needed everyone else to validate my worth. Those were my insecurity issues. I'm not saying that every time our stomach is upset we are experiencing self-doubt. I'm not saying that at all. What I am saying is if there is a consistent pattern of this behavior in any of the above, you may want to ask yourself the big question: What am I afraid of that is causing me such anxiety? I believe that once we get beyond our fears, we can live a life of freedom.

Most of the time we are not operating in our own truth, therefore the lies we have told society stagnate our walk. We must always show up in the world wearing our truth. Sometimes society isn't thrilled about the truth we tell, but we must get past altering our lives for the sake of being popular. My mom always told me that if you tell the truth in the beginning, it doesn't matter how much time passes, you will always remember your truth. What I realize is truth will release you from bondage. Bondage that has had us on lockdown for years, generation after generation.

On April 6, 2016, in Kansas City, Missouri, I entered the sanctuary and stood before 159 women, sharing my mess with family, friends, and peers. I stood in my truth being transparent about every angle of my life. The life that many didn't know existed was revealed. Later, I shared my truth with the world in my first book, *From Being Kept to Being Kept*. When you walk in your truth there is a sense of BOLD humility that comes out in a place of sincerity to all.

As you pick up the pieces and walk in your truth, you must be in alignment with God. My life was so out of alignment with Christ I didn't even know how lost I was. It was clear that on the outside, everything looked great, but I was completely lost in my own being.

As you turn the pages of this book, prepare your mind, body, and soul for a journey of truth. A journey that has allowed each of us to strategically pick up each shattered piece of glass and create our very own beautiful masterpiece. I am looking forward to hearing about yours.

Love,

Rochinda

Chapter 2

The First Step

Get up and go to your mirror right now. And if you are not near a mirror, I presume you have your phone handy. Look into that mirror or activate the camera on your phone so you can see your face and look deep into your eyes. Erase all the background noise of life out of your mind. Take this one moment for you. However uncomfortable, take this moment to look deep into your own spirit. Once you have tuned out all of the hustle and bustle of the world, focus on yourself for this moment in time. Repeat after me, "I am taking the first step."

Your divine purpose in life is to live at your maximum potential.

Your divine purpose in life is to live at your maximum potential. Let me just take a moment to level the playing field for all those whose eyes grace these pages. Each and every one of you are a magnificent existence. Say that aloud,

"I am a Magnificent Existence!" I can't hear you. Say it again, "I am a Magnificent Existence." Yes, that's better.

Do you know there is no one else like your unique self? Your thoughts, your time in space, your divineness was created from the Divine. From before you were a being, God knew your place and task in this world, and He had a mission assigned to you and your magnificent existence. Even as you sit reading this book, you are in motion taking multiple steps per minute. All the more evidence to validate your magnificent existence. In your core, your heart is beating to circulate blood to your organs. Your lungs are in motion to inhale and exhale, to perfuse your tissues with oxygen so you can think and move your muscles to navigate through life.

Delving deeper into the innate motion that exists within you, think about reading this book. Your eyes are seeing the words, and faster than the speed of light, your nerve endings within your eyes transmit the words to your brain, and your brain interprets the words to your mind to determine the understanding of what you are reading. You can see, up close and personal, what you are made of and more importantly, whose you are. You are a magnificent existence.

You may be wondering, what at all, if anything, does this have to do with taking the first step? I am showing you that you were made for motion. You were made for taking steps. And, all motion starts with taking the first step. The first step can be scary and cause anxiety that overwhelms your spirit. However, we must hold 2 Timothy 1:7 in the forefront of our minds, "For God did not give us a spirit of fear, but of power and love and of a sound mind." When doubt and negativity flood your head, speak that verse aloud. Let your eyes see that prophetic word, while your ears hear the words prophesy over your life.

> *"God was taking things out of me and putting tools into me for me to fulfill my purpose."*

Also lean on Philippians 4:8, "Finally, brothers and sisters, whatever is true, whatever is noble, whatever is right, whatever is pure, whatever is lovely, whatever is admirable, think about such things." Enrobe yourself in these promises of God as you take your first step.

January 2016, I decided to make a vision board. I had not done that in a while, and I figured it would be the best way to visualize and put into motion everything God had placed in my spirit. I found the word "GO" on a page in the magazine and was instantly connected with the word because God kept placing in my spirit, "GO!" I felt it was God speaking to me and confirming what I was to do. I placed that word in the middle of my black vision board as the foundation for what I was seeing. I knew this was a word from God.

A couple of days later, I was invited to a motivational empowerment event. At the close of the event, I ran into a pastor that leads one of the churches that visited my home church regularly. In the middle of asking about my parents and family back home, he said the Holy Spirit had given him a prophetic word to share with me and told me the Holy Spirit said I should,

"Go, Go, Go!" He went on to say, "God was taking things out of me and putting tools into me for me to fulfill my purpose."

Besides being amazed at how the word from God aligned with what I believed God had told me, it was confirmation for my spirit. And I speak that confirmation over each and every one of you reading this book. "Go" into your day with purpose and intention. Each day you will become closer and closer to your destiny and purpose. However, in order to "Go," you must take the first step. You already have the motion within you. Now it is time to match that internal motion with the external and take the first step, because you are a magnificent existence.

Conventionally, as a society, we think of our lives from beginning to end. We are born, we grow up, we become adults, and we age. However, I believe God thinks of us from our ending to the beginning. I imagine that God has a notebook and a pen in which he uses to write in this notebook. With that pen, he writes out the divine purpose of all the beings He created. Certain things have been written in pen, like the love He has for us. The forgiveness He has for us, and the salvation that is readily available for all of us, if we choose.

When I think of something written in pen, I imagine its finality. That's why I am so glad God's love is final for all of us. Assured of that security, I pray you release all your fears and know that your purpose is already written by the almighty hand of God. I pray you

will step out on faith, trusting that if you heed God's voice, you are well able to walk into your purpose. You are a magnificent existence, take the first step.

As we drive throughout our perspective cities, we often pass by places of rest or cemeteries. Within those cemeteries are headstones. And on those headstones are dates of birth and dates of transition. What separates those distinct times are a dash. That dash represents all of the movement an individual had within their life. It represents all of the purposes fulfilled and all those purposes that were not. And we are declaring and decreeing today in this moment that we are coming against any and everything that attempts to keep us from our true magnificent existence.

By taking the first step, you are staring anxiety in the face and rebuking the unknown. Most importantly, you are acknowledging that you are God's child and He is going to see you through. By taking the first step, you bind all negative thoughts trying to creep into the corners of your mind. By taking the first step, you seek God's counsel and create a covenant with the Holy Spirit for your destiny, canceling out the plans the enemy had to stumble you. In addition, you realize that to take the first step, you cannot be complacent. You have to take charge of the gifts God has entrusted to you.

By taking the first step, you are destiny bound to defy the odds the enemy has orchestrated against you. You cancel all doubt, because there is no room for doubt in taking the first step. By taking the first step, you evolve into the new creature God intended you to be and embrace your untouched destiny. By taking the first step, you find yourself on a beautiful journey while figuring out that God did not make any mistakes. By taking the first step, you come into full understanding that you are God's cherished possession and genocide of your purpose is no longer an option.

> *By taking the first step, you will know when to lead and when to find a leader to lead you.*

By taking the first step, you profess you have what it takes, and you halt everyone and everything in your path from hindering you. By taking the first step, you ignore those stinking inner thoughts and learn to ignite your own power within. By taking the first step, you jump for joy at each little victory along the way. By taking the first step, you will know the innate knowledge God has placed in your inner core is part of your infinite purpose. By taking the first step, you will know when to lead and when to find a leader to lead you.

Reassured of God's love and His confirmation that you did not need what you felt you lost along the way, you will learn to let go and trust that God has something better for you. By taking the first step, you understand that you indeed are a magnificent existence. You understand with your whole heart that you are more than enough, and God has put everything in you

that you need. All of us that are members of humanity have a brain, two eyes, one nose, one mouth, one heart, and two lungs. And this is all you need to take the first step.

By taking the first step, you will not give up when you fall off track. And in case you did not catch the newsflash, nothing or no one is better than you or has more purpose than you. God has given us all a perfect measure. What the Divine expects from you is praise, honor, and nothing less than what He planted in you. By taking the first step, you will fully evaluate all options and be prayerful about which direction to pursue. By taking the first step, you will know that a consistent prayer life is key.

By taking the first step, you vow to quit putting off the first step. By taking the first step, you recognize that God will put the right people in place at the right time, and you have to reconcile with everything you have placed in your mental basement. You reconcile with it, but you do not relive it. Acknowledge all the hurt and pain and all the ways you have felt slighted, reconcile it, own the lesson life wants to teach you and move on. By taking the first step, you sacrifice holding on to lost dreams and ambition. That is not an option anymore.

As you traverse through life, who you should share your dreams with will come to you by prayer and supplication, but, don't cast you pearls before swine (Matthew 7:6). With God's help, you will be able to know when it is time to glean from someone, when to

mentor and when to be mentored to. By taking the first step, you understand that you sit at the Father's feet. Each step after the first step puts you on the other side of victory. Victory is simply being one step closer to the end result. Each step is a victory. By taking the first step, winning is in your being, in your thought process.

By taking the first step, you x-ray your surroundings, looking deeply into the company you are keeping. If they are not aligned with the promises of God, reprioritize their influence in your life. By taking the first step, you understand you must take care of yourself. Your body is your vessel, and it is the only vessel you get. If the vessel is not attended to, then one would think it can impact how God can use you. Get your checkups, be compliant with your medications, and most of all, move that vessel. Exercise.

You are already a being in motion inside, match that with motion on the outside. You are a vessel, and you have to be available to be used by God. By taking the first step, realize God has placed you in a zone of fulfillment. Embrace being in that zone. Let God work on you in that space. There will be ups and downs, however, you have to be steadfast and hold on to your faith. In that zone, you will want to get with likeminded people. The phrase, "iron sharpens iron," is true. There is also a common phrase that if you are the smartest one in your circle, maybe you should consider getting a new circle. In order to walk in your purpose, you will need to be strong and sharp, and you will need to be in a circle that is aligned with the Holy Spirit.

We are all busy with work, children, and spouses. When the thought crosses your mind that you do not have time to take the first step to start that business, write that book, or develop that business plan, just know that time is a gift from the Almighty. In fact, time is your innate commerce. Time is the one thing we are all born with that levels the playing field. We all have the same twenty-four hours in a day. You do have the time, you do have the smarts, and you do have everything you need to take the first step.

As we take our first steps together, and the momentum comes from the steps that follow, I beckon you to look for the full circle moments. There will be full circle moments that come right away, and those that take a little longer to come into fruition. I also like to reference them as my G3 moments-God's Grace and Glory Moments. And what I challenge you to do is to pay attention, notice those moments, and glorify God in those moments and be in God's presence to truly worship and give a high praise for what you have gone through to get to that moment. It may be that you had to ride the bus that would pass by a car dealership, and then you are able to buy a car in that lot. It may be that you used to drive through a neighborhood and dream of having a house there, and then are able to hold the keys in your hand to a house in that neighborhood. Those are full circle moments or G3 moments-a representation of God's Grace and Glory. When that happens recognize it and honor it! I'll give you a personal example of a full circle-G3 moment for me. When I was a little girl in the second grade, I was traveling through Topeka, Kansas. And we stopped at the state capitol. A small group of us went on a tour of the state capitol. I was in awe of the tall columns, the marble floors, and the copper bannisters. I thought to myself, that this was a very special place. And last week I had the privilege to be a speaker at a meeting in that very same building, for me, that was a special G3 full circle moment.

Recognizing those moments validates your momentum and is a direct result of taking the first step.

Before you read this book, you probably referred to yourself as "me" when referencing yourself. From this day forward, I encourage you to redefine yourself. Yes, you can still refer to yourself as "me", with the understanding that me means you are a <u>magnificent existence</u>, and you are fully capable of taking the first step to fulfill who God deems you to be. God's eye is on the sparrow, and you know He is watching over you. Get up, put one foot in front of the other and take the first step.

Dr. Teresa M. Wesley is a physician, motivational speaker, health moderator and author. As a physician and motivational speaker, Dr.

Wesley promotes the empowerment of individuals by encouraging them to be steadfast in holding on to their vision, faith and resilience. Dr. Wesley has keen insight into the amazing concepts that empower individuals to lead balanced and magnificent existence lives. Dr. Wesley is the author of her self- published book, "Vision, Faith, and Resilience", which is a strong collection of both motivational and inspirational accounts that assist individuals through the challenges that life presents. Dr. Wesley is also a co- contributor to *100 Words of Wisdom for Women, a 31 day Exercise in Empowerment,* which invites the reader to be fully engaged in discovering themselves towards the path of empowerment. Dr. Wesley, is a devoted wife and mother, and knows that her steps are ordered by the Lord. She also s believes that this current collaborative project, Picking Up The Pieces, will have a dynamic impact all of the readers of the book.

Chapter 3

Silent Affliction

I grew up in Southeast Kansas City, Missouri as one of sixteen children. My birth spot lands me right in the middle of two sets of kids, an older set and a younger set. My mother worked full-time as a nurse at a local hospital and my father was a disc jockey at multiple night clubs. Momma had a lot of mouths to feed so she spent a lot of time at the hospital earning a living, and she did just that. She provided without much financial support from my father, even though he was in the home. Like everyone else, with the exception of a few families, I grew up in a dysfunctional home. My mother and father are still married today. My father made a very large family, but he wasn't exactly a family man if you know what I mean. He was a disc jockey in various nightclubs in the seventies and eighties, and he loved the nightlife. I was pretty much raised by my older brothers and sisters who were still kids themselves. I was not raised in a "nurturing environment," but, who is when children are raising children?

As a child I very much went against the grain. The best way to get me to do something was to tell me not to do it. Needless to say, that always landed me in

trouble. My mom used to say to me, "You just got to learn things the hard way, don't you?" And, I did.

What you don't know can hurt you, unfortunately.

I knew my mom prayed because I always heard her say, "Lord have mercy on me." To whom she prayed, I did not know. Early in my teenage years, I decided I didn't want to believe in God. My mind couldn't fathom the thought of an imaginary man in the sky, a puppet master who controls everything. Forget that! And, there was no changing my mind about it. Period.

What intrigued me and caught my interest were things like the paranormal, ghost stories, ouija boards, Bloody Mary. You know? The dark stuff kids get curious about. Those things didn't scare me. I never even had a nightmare. I was naive in my curiosity, and it proved to have grave consequences.

At fifteen, I ran across some books about the occult and the supernatural. I didn't really know what they were "per se." I just knew it could be scary, and I wanted to see what it was. I was excited to read any spooky stories I might come across. Unbeknownst to me, one of those books wasn't just any book. It was the Satanic Bible. It didn't read like a satanic anything to me, and at the time I thought nothing of it.

What you don't know can hurt you, unfortunately. When you read and indulge in things like that, it takes your mind to a dark place and then at night when you go to sleep, your mind is still in that dark place. I had opened a door I didn't know existed. So, of course, I did not know how to close it either.

I went from never having had a nightmare to living a nightmare.

Things started to happen, subtly. A little bad dream progressed into nightmares. Not just regular, "oh, I had a bad dream" nightmares, they were more like night terrors. My life changed drastically. I was not getting any sleep. I was afraid to close my eyes because I had monsters in my head. What's worse, I started seeing those same "monsters" in the mirrors. I went from never having had a nightmare to living a nightmare. I couldn't get away from the monsters whether I was asleep or awake.

I felt myself losing grip on reality and sliding down a slippery slope of despair. There was no peace. I was being tormented in the confines of my mind. I tried to tell anyone who would listen that I was having these nightmares, but they would respond, "I'm sorry you're not sleeping well." Besides, who would believe something so bizarre?

The experience was making me crazy. I knew I couldn't just tell anybody that I was seeing faces and hearing voices. I only told a select few about that part. I would have gotten locked up for sure. So, I endured it. I was convinced there was nothing anybody could do to make the monsters stop. The state of fear and paranoia I lived in intensified to the point where I didn't want to live anymore.

I tried to kill myself. The voices in my head coached me on how to do it. They taunted me, telling me no one would care that I was gone, that no one would even notice. I took a bottle of pills while sitting in a crowded room. Sadly, they were right. No one even noticed. I didn't die of course, and the voices never left. I felt alone and isolated. These experiences went on for over a year.

One day, I ran into a friend I used to hang out with. She knew I was severely depressed, so I told her what was going on with me. She said, "The devil has plans for you, girl!" "That's not helping me," I cried. I thought my cries fell on deaf ears, but she said, "I'm going to take you to see my pastor."

Although I didn't believe in God, if this God and pastor could make the nightmares, voices, and faces in the mirror stop, I was all for going. At that point, I was willing to try just about anything.

> *One day, I had a divine intervention. The Son of God was waiting for me in my bedroom.*

My friend kept her word. She picked me up and took me to her pastor. She must have briefed him on my situation before we arrived because he didn't ask a bunch of questions. He only asked, "Do you accept Jesus Christ to be your Lord and Savior?" "Yes." I lied. I was desperate.

We joined hands, and he prayed for me. I don't know what he prayed. I was there in body, but mentally, I was absent. I went deaf. I really didn't know what was going on. After he finished praying, I opened my eyes and things didn't seem any different. But when I went home, I slept without nightmares for the first time in almost two years. I was elated.

I still wasn't completely in the clear. My tormentors were no longer in my head, but they were still in our house. I moved out and about a year later, that house caught on fire and burned down.

No More Excuses

I had been delivered and snatched out of the clutches of Satan's grip. Hallelujah, who knew? I survived an insidious situation. I told you I have to learn things the hard way. I'm so glad I was wrong about God. Not only is there a God, but He is alive and not dead. God to me is not a belief. I know there is a God who loves us. God is so good, He sent his son Jesus for me, literally. I was so lost, He left his flock to find me. I am the lost sheep.

One day, I had a divine intervention. The Son of God was waiting for me in my bedroom. I heard a Voice. Uh, oh, here we go again. But this time it was different. It wasn't like the voices I had heard before. This voice was inside my head and audible to my ears. This voice didn't bring fear and anguish. He was love. He said, "We've been waiting for you!"

I could feel His excitement when He spoke to me. His presence engulfed me. I could feel His glory from the top of my head to the bottom of my feet, inside, outside, through and through. I struggle to articulate my experience because we lack the vocabulary to accurately describe it. It felt like love, bliss, elation, and jubilee all at once. I basked in His abounding love. I couldn't believe the Son of God was excited about me.

"Why?" I questioned Him. He said, "Because I love you!" Like a little kid, I said, "You do?" He replied, "Yes! I've always loved you, even before you were formed in your mother's womb. We love all of creation! None more, none less. All the same. It's okay to be who you are as long as it is in truth." He accepted me, even though I denied Him. He was oh, so gentle, tender and kind. He didn't judge me, chastise me, or push me away. He comforted me and allowed me to rest in Him.

He is my security and protector. He said, "You are equipped with everything you need to live this Human Experience. You were created that way. You have the ability to exercise your control. You live in a world that is against you, but you have another enemy first, even before the evil one. It's you. You are enemy number one. If God is for you then who can be against you?" The word says, "The battle has already been won."

I knew I was responsible for the chaos I had caused in my life. Yet and still, He encouraged me to live a life without regrets. He forgave me and remembered my sins no more. He gave me a new heart and a new spirit. Jesus is sufficient. He is exceedingly and abundantly greater than we could ever imagine. You will never understand the Creator of the world with your intellectual mind for He is far too great for your brain to conceive.

It doesn't matter who you are or what you have done, you are not exempt from the Father's Love. He is able to do all things, and He is willing to be your help when you are in need. Call on the name of Jesus. You can go to Him for all that concerns you, even if you caused the problem yourself. Do not make God your last resort. Make Him your only resort in the mighty name of Jesus. Amen!

Shikara Rodriquez is a devoted wife, mother and grandmother. It is her desire to encourage and inspire others to seek a relationship with the Most High God through his son, Jesus Christ. She has spoken at various conferences, churches, and gatherings around the Kansas City area. Her testimony can be seen on YouTube: "The Truth" talk show "Shakira's Testimony." She is affiliated with several Ministries including Mercy Chose Me Ministry (MCMM), The Whole Truth Ministry, and I Thirst Ministry. She strives to touch the lives and hearts of many by sharing the love of God with all who will listen.

Chapter 4

Paralyzed

Divorced in Mid-Life: But Still Standing

Did he think I would crumble and not bounce back after he solemnly swore he would love me no matter what until death do we part? I remember his words so clearly. He said, "Divorce is not an option."

I was married for nine years, but my husband and I lived together for a year prior to saying our wedding vows in front of a minister, family and friends. *At Last* by Etta James played as I walked toward my soon-to- be husband. I felt so safe and certain that love had come along, and this marriage would be everlasting. In the beginning of our relationship, we struggled with barriers I erected to prevent others from

This is about how I went from a life in full bloom to a shipwreck.

getting too close to me. I had trust issues regarding men in general, and the barrier protected my heart from getting broken by others, especially men.

With him, I had lowered the barrier before I realized it. And, for the first time in my life, I allowed this man, who would eventually become my husband, to get close to me. As a result, I was able to unmask and reveal that I too wanted to be accepted and loved unconditionally. I felt very certain that my heart would be handled with extreme care. I honestly believed he would live up to his words, which were to love me unconditionally, protect me and provide for me. For the first time in my life, I wholeheartedly trusted a male figure. Since I trusted him, the most important people in my life trusted him as well.

This is not intended to bring about any ill feelings on this man whom I entrusted my life to and thought of as my protector. This is about how I went from a life in full bloom to a shipwreck. And how I was able to survive the storm and the multiple aftershocks with the help of God in spite of my losses. This is about being able to stand and developing an encouraging outlook for my life.

Minutes before I learned my marriage was doomed, I had talked with my husband on the drive home, like always. Our communication was good, there was absolutely nothing out of the ordinary. I had been in the house less than ten minutes when something told me to look out the window. To my surprise, I saw a car pull up in the driveway behind my parked vehicle. I immediately opened the door, and my world came crashing down as I was served divorce papers. Dumbfounded and totally confused, I thought for sure there had been some mistake. My world slowed. Everything blurred. I felt like I died in that

moment, and God resuscitated me and carried me until I was able to stand on my own. I don't recall much after receiving the divorce papers. I know I called my mother, and she told me to be strong, that I could get through this.

Instead, I spent the next several months going through the motions of living.

Sometimes in life certain things happen and at the time it may not make much sense as to why it happened. The termination of my marriage was like this. Some people said, "It was God that put you two together." One of my sisters described my husband as my "knight in shining armor." She said we were like, "Will and Jada (Smith)." She had such great hope for us. Prior to divorce papers being served, everything seemed fine. I am not saying we had a perfect marriage, but we talked and laughed with each other. We had just come back from a trip. He even initiated plans to celebrate my birthday in August. There was nothing out of the ordinary. I never suspected that by September, my marriage would be dissolved. When I asked when was this decided and why, no straight-forward explanation was offered. In fact, I have never received any solid explanation for why our marriage ended. And with no answers, I struggled for a long time with finding closure.

When I received the news that our marriage was being tossed away, it felt as if my heart had been stabbed with a very sharp knife that was pushed in as far as it could go. I bled for months. I felt paralyzed, and I struggled with how to pick up the shattered pieces and move forward. I was so wounded during this hurtful ordeal. It felt as though I had multiple wounds throughout my body that no doctor could heal. I was drowning in so many emotions and regret. I wanted to escape reality, disengage from society and avoid all the questions from others. But I couldn't. Instead, I spent the next several months going through the motions of living.

I went into "warrior" mode. I only had a few semesters left to complete my degree and I was determined to finish. With my husband's encouragement to go back to school, I had been working diligently to complete this milestone and obtain my Master's. He always seemed excited for me to reach this goal, and alongside my daughter, I labeled him my biggest supporter. But right in the middle of my Master's program, my world was turned upside down and I was presented with this life-changing event.

While going through the divorce and for many months afterwards, my inner voice worked overtime with all the whys and what ifs. I thought back to other couples that were constantly fighting, had major financial problems or faced infidelity and had remained married. As far as I knew, that was not our situation. I became exhausted trying to figure out what happened. Besides work, my daughter and grandbabies, I went *Looking through the lens shattered by turmoil, I could not see beyond my pain.* into isolation and began to self-medicate. I developed anxieties about growing old and being alone, wasting time, figuring out how to divide my time with school and work, finances, retirement, how to keep masking so others would think I was doing just fine and most of all, re-erecting my barrier so I would never have to trust again.

Amid the turmoil, I forced myself to attend classes, finish multiple research papers and make presentations. Finally, I reached a point where I could no longer push myself, and I did the unspeakable. I shared with my professor that I was going through a divorce and was having a difficult time staying focused. He gave me permission to take the semester off and that is what I did.

When I hit the lowest low, I had had enough. With tears rolling down my face, I screamed out to God, "I just want to die." This was far from the truth. I just wanted my life as I knew it for the past ten years back. I was embarrassed, and I felt like such a failure to be going through my third divorce. Yes, third divorce. I was disappointed that I had trusted a man and even angrier that I had lost ten years of my life. I began to ponder Maya Angelou's words, "Don't lose your pretty." I started to compare how I was prior to being married, younger and less conservative. I was certain the devil was doing a happy dance with thinking that he had won my soul.

When I was not working, I spent most of my time alone, soul searching and reflecting on various times in my life. What lesson was God trying to teach me? I thought back on the other marriages I had walked away from. I wondered if this was what it meant to reap what you sow or was my husband reaping what he sowed, and I just got caught in the crossfire. Maybe this was a reality check because I had put so much faith in this man to protect and care for me. I deactivated my Facebook account to keep from seeing everybody else's perfect life on display. I didn't want to talk to anyone about my divorce.

Always in thought, I had become the "Great Thinker." But I stopped trying to understand why and allowed myself space to accept what was. Sometimes there are no answers. I leaned into the notion that I am perfectly made by God (Matthew 5:48), and I knew I would eventually soar away from this mess. Occasionally, I went to the church we had attended throughout our marriage. But it soon felt awkward, especially when I saw people who knew us both. I found comfort in reading the bible. One inspiring verse found in 2 Chronicles 20:15, "The battle is not yours but God's," helped me tremendously. When I gave this "divorce issue" to God, it was the start of my healing journey. Before, I was asking, "Why me?" Now, I am saying, "Why not me?" Looking through the lens

shattered by turmoil, I could not see beyond my pain. I didn't understand why this happened.

In 2006, my son died, and it was so heartbreaking. His death was very difficult for me. I now believe God placed this man in my life for a season to help me endure the pain of the loss of my son. God knew when He took my son to be with Him that I would think He had forsaken me, and I did. I see now that my now ex-husband was in my life for that period as I was grieving the loss of my son. Today, I have actually thanked my ex-husband for being there during that painful time of losing my child. I now know that God did not leave me. He was with me then, and He is with me now. The Bible says, "God is with you and will never forsake you" (Deuteronomy 31:6). God has taken me on this journey for a reason. I recall my mother always saying that God is not going to put more on you than you can handle (1 Corinthians 10:13).

> Today, my faith is much stronger, and I am confident in knowing who really walks with me.

My prayer is that God will use me to help other women who are going through life changing events, such as a divorce. Today, my faith is much stronger, and I am confident in knowing who really walks with me. Everything I went through was not for me to understand, so I have stopped wasting my energy trying to figure things out. Energy wasted only slows down the progression of moving forward and receiving what God has planned for your life.

There is life after divorce. I obtained my Master's degree. And yes, I am still standing. Storms will come, but having faith and staying prayed up will help you get through. I believe the worst things that happen in our lives can align us with a path we can journey down to achieve our greatest potential.

Life is a journey. There are many roads one must travel to get to their destination, with lots of twists and turns. T.D. Jakes said in one of his sermons, "God is going to recalculate the route and get you back on track." God is recalculating my route, so I can achieve my purpose in life. I challenge anyone who is going through a life changing ordeal that causes them to feel paralyzed and defeated, "Give it to God and let Him work it out."

Marsha Aka-Bashorun was born in Kansas City, Missouri,

currently she lives in Oklahoma City. She is a mother of two, grandmother of three and a friend to many. She received her Bachelor of Science Degree in Family Life Education/ Gerontology and Master Degree in Gerontology from the University of Central Oklahoma. She is an advocate for the aging population. She is the CEO of "You Are Beautiful Foundation". Her passion runs deep with encouraging ladies to understand, that although there will be challenges the key to achieving your goal is to keep pushing forward".

Chapter 5

Divine Instructions

Looking up into the sky with all my might, I attempt to reach it. My stomach tickles as I arch my back, glide back down, and kick my legs into the air with full exuberance. This is my second and third attempt at being one with the resting place of a myriad of stars. It is perfectly clear, not a cloud in sight, as I sway back and forth in my swing. My eyes are captivated by this endless blue that captures me every time. In this moment, my biggest hope is that the leather seat which cups me securely at the end of this thick rusty chain does not stop its back and forth motion as it propels me into the air. I've made up a rule, in my overactive mind that I could not jump out of the swing until it comes to a complete

> *It is not unusual for me to be far away from my physical self—in my head questioning, wondering, and analyzing the world.*

stop. In the distance, I hear the school bell ringing and children's laughter as their footsteps hit the concrete in response to the principal's call for us to come inside. I don't move. I just sit here lost in my thoughts. It is not unusual for me to be far away from my physical self—in my head--questioning, wondering, and analyzing the world. Why is the sky blue? How far away is it from the ground? How can it be day light here and dark elsewhere? How does that work, exactly? How is it that the moon, the stars, and the sun are supposed to be so large, yet appear so small? And where is this God who made the world and everything in it? Is He up there looking down at me right now? Can He hear my every thought? These are just a few of the thousand and one questions clanging around in my inquisitive, young mind.

My little girl dream to own the secret of what kept the schoolyard swing in perpetual motion was never realized. Perhaps if it had been, my impending forlorn years could have been avoided. But at what cost? Time passed. I grew up, graduated high school, entered adulthood, left home, married, divorced, married again, and divorced…once again.

When the return on investment from wearing the last two surnames as though they were badges of honor came back null and void, what I wanted more than ever was my birth name back. My frustration and disappointment with life, myself, and the bad choices I had made caused me to question everything, especially my identity. I didn't know who I was, but I knew I was born a Berry. And like a drowning person desperately needing to attach themselves to an anchor, I needed to reattach myself to who I was born to be. I wasn't sure what I wanted in life, but I was certain I wasn't living. Although it seemed unattainable, I craved purposeful, intentional, fulfilled living.

Sure, I was breathing. I interacted with family and friends and even returned to school, earning a Bachelor of Arts in Management and Human Relations. I attended church regularly, volunteered my time, and was

I was terrified of failing and beyond doubtful about who I thought God had called me to be.

involved in extracurricular activities, all while striving to be a good wife and holding down a job…many jobs.

Discontentment followed me to every single one, leaving me drained, depleted and on the hunt for my next unsuccessful attempt at staving off boredom while being a responsible citizen to society. One day at work, I recall watching my co-workers engage in office chatter, seemingly quite content as they buzzed around the busy office. It was as though I was spying on them through a telescope and their voices seemed far away. I could hear my own voice saying, "Surely they are pretending to be happy. Why am I so miserable, and they're not? What's wrong with me?" I felt as though I was suffocating. That evening as I drove home, I cried like a hungry baby in need of a diaper change. Thank God it was daylight savings time, because the darkness kept my secret. This was one of several occasions where I felt deep remorse for the many paths I had chosen in life, especially in my vocation.

I was terrified of failing and beyond doubtful about who I thought God had called me to be. I repeatedly chose disobedience and settled out of fear, which created a cycle of applying for and accepting positions that were, at least for me, remedial at best. I envisioned myself doing all the things God created me to do and be. Yet somehow, I had made up in my mind that it was simply that, an idea made up in my mind. The inquisitive little girl from so long ago remained. She had never left. Her lack of nurture, spiritual counsel, confidence and guidance morphed her into an adult who emulated the practices and behaviors of the lives played out before her as a child instead of seeking the answers she needed. Instead of yielding to the voice she had heard countless times, prompting her to go in a certain direction, she allowed fear and doubt to nudge her onto a path that led her further away from the gifts and talents which made up her true self. She leaned more into the voices of others whom she could see, instead of listening to the quiet, yet distinct, still voice from the Entity she could not see. And because of that, there were consequences.

God created us with purpose on purpose (Exodus 9:16). There's not always a clearly defined answer or roadmap. However, in obedience, we are to put one foot in front of the other, practicing faith and trust, which will manifest itself in our actions. Our faith will come by hearing and studying the word of God (Romans 10:17). Like the branches of a tree that bend with no resistance when the wind blows, we are to go in the direction God calls us, with no resistance. But then there is free will—to choose our own paths. Yet the fallen world we are born into exposes me and you to sin, which comprises much fallout onto the innocent. Over forty years ago, that sensitive, smart, curious, Holy Spirit filled little girl was created for greatness. She was made to know God intimately and then share His love with others.

Without pointing the finger at any person, because of an obvious void in my upbringing as the youngest of seven children raised by a single mom, I didn't know who I was in God. Therefore, I doubted my purpose. Yet my heart was steadfast—always believing that God had so much more for me. But it was easier—more comfortable—to allow my flesh to lead and win the ongoing battle, keeping me immobilized from my customized path. Fast forward to now, after countless mistakes, heartaches, heartbreaks and pain, God's grace has truly been sufficient. When God has started a good work in us, it will be completed (Philippians 1:6).

> *The memories of my time spent at church less than a mile away from my childhood home are vivid.*

As far back as I can remember, I preferred reading or writing over the popular pastime of watching television or chatting on the phone with friends as most of my sisters did. Oddly enough, my attention was drawn to lecturers who provided information or preachers who read from the Bible on the religious channel. On Sunday mornings, while at church, I could literally burst from absorbing the words that spilled from the pastor's mouth. Half speaking and half singing the sermon, he'd pace up and down the center aisle all dressed up in his satin gold robe with red sash. The atmosphere pregnant with sounds of singing, humming and shouting. Tears that were impossible to hold back fell from my eyes as I clapped my hands with conviction. My counterparts would either be drawing on paper their parents gave them to keep quiet or crying because they didn't understand my tears and didn't know what else to do. As an adult, I experience the same joy when praising the Lord on Sunday mornings that I felt as a young person. That's how I know it was not mere emotion. It was the Spirit that came from the Father Himself, rested upon my soul. The same Spirit now dwells within me and is more determined to get my attention so I might practice obedience, spreading God's love and message that He is real.

The memories of my time spent at church less than a mile away from my childhood home are vivid. Sure, there were times I preferred not to be a part of the roll count on Sunday mornings, but before the choir was done with their first chorus, I was on my feet with the adults encapsulated in an indescribable feeling. As poignant to my spirit as the music was that poured from the church organ, I was saddened and more deeply affected for the pedestrians I could see outside the church window strolling aimlessly up and down the side street. I saw them as lost, clearly unaware of the goings on inside the small, corner Baptist church.

I was a sensitive child in every definition of the word. When another experienced any type of intense feelings—pain or joy—it was as though I was physically connected to their heart equally sharing in that emotion. My gift of empathy allows me to discern the disposition of others and to know things that have never been told to me. My mom made us attend Sunday school and church.

And sometimes, when she was caught up on her sleep after working double shifts, she would attend with us. But to say we were raised in a religious household would be a significant stretch. Our neighborhood consisted more of families who shunned church than those who went to church. My siblings were too caught up in their own adolescent and teenage affairs to be aware of their baby sister's inquiries of the world and the "phenomena" of God and religious practices. Except for the few times my brother took me and my sister to a predominantly white church outside the neighborhood by bus and my eldest sister's periodic nudging for me to pray at bedtime, there was no strong spiritual influence or guidance. The desire to read the entire Bible while lying belly down on the shellac wooden floor of the bedroom I shared with two of my sisters came not from my surroundings or outside of myself. It came from within, where it was birthed before I was born into this fallen world.

One could then ask, "How was such a calling rejected?" How could divine instructions from the Lord be ignored? Certainly, valid questions when hindsight provides clarity in how the Holy Spirit rested on me as a little girl. Without strong pillars to uphold me, it was impossible to recognize any of my spiritual gifts or calling on my life. Sure, I had all the necessities to grow physically, but there was a huge deficit of positive role models to assist in guidance, which thwarted my spiritual and emotional growth.

During my impressionable years, I floundered in a sea of limited thinking, insecurity, and unworthiness, which resulted in low self-esteem and lack of direction. Doubt and fear of failure riddled my entire being leaving me dejected and unmotivated to walk into my calling. I was like a lost boat floating aimlessly without an oar to help in guiding me away from the sea of lies and destruction that nearly muffled out God's promises for my life. I began to believe that I was a part of my environment, and what others said about me I took as truth, more than what I felt in my heart and soul what God said about me.

After trying to find love in ALL the wrong places—failing at two marriages, resigning to an ideology of others about who I was, what I should think, say, and do, AND questioning God's voice while upholding a rebellious spirit against God's instruction--I spiraled into a state of depression and an overwhelming feeling

> *If you glean nothing else from this chapter, know that God is real, and He loves you immensely.*

of "being stuck." Where I needed to be for God to get my full attention was in a dark place where no person could assist. In this dark place, where excruciating pain of being rejected by others and feeling lost literally brought me to my knees, God's light began to penetrate the doomed pit. And through His written Word, He spoke with gentle assurance, providing a comfort that could come from no other place or being. The Holy Spirit reminded my broken self that I could be healed through the medicinal effect of His power and scripture after scripture spoke to my wounded soul, resulting in the beginning of my healing process. To assist me in disciplined study, God was intentional in blessing me with divine connections within an isolated environment that He divinely orchestrated to allow razor sharp focus on His Word. My journey to wholeness began when God allowed me to crumble under His watchful eyes, believing I would find my way back piece by piece.

If you glean nothing else from this chapter, know that God is real, and He loves you immensely. Just as He continuously whispered in my ear from childhood to come to Him, I'm certain if you think back, He has revealed His presence to you too, perhaps in a more prominent way. Did you answer? Will you answer? The purpose He put in each one of us, which will never depart, is ultimately to glorify Him. But if we part from it, know that it is not of God to jump ship. He will wait, coax, and guide us back into His will for our lives. We are called to hear and obey our specific divine instructions.

Walking in boldness requires confidence that we hear the instructions with clarity. Confirmation is received by studying and meditating on scripture, coupled with praying and fasting. Supernaturally, pristine understanding of His commandments will transform us into His likeness and our desires will match His desires for our lives. And even with this, the face of doubt may turn to taunt us from time to time. It is then that I would encourage you to not entertain for a moment what could immobilize progression towards your purpose. Instead, aggressively seek God's face by turning back to His promise, which will establish you and provide reassurance to keep pressing forward.

If it were left up to the little girl from long ago, you would find her still lost in the blueness of that perfect clear sky. But glory to God and all His wisdom, although He extends free will allowing us to choose our own journey, when we become lost His hand is not far from our reach, ready to guide us back to Him. Find peace in knowing that as we listen and obey our divine instructions, even if the next step on our journey is obscure, it will land solid because God ordains it.

Carlotta Berry is a native of Kansas City, MO and the youngest of seven children. Her educational background includes a Bachelor's degree in  Management and Human Relations from Mid America Nazarene University in Olathe KS. She graduated with the class of 2005. Ms. Berry has a heart for God and is passionate about spreading the true and beloved message of God's existence and love through poetry. As a child, she has always best expressed herself through writing and dreamt of becoming a published author. The Holy Spirit has ignited her gift of inspirational writing which provides hope to those in "darkness" and on the brink of giving up. She enjoys running, the outdoors, and loves animals. She is the proud owner of an 11-year-old poodle mix named Jade. The Kept Woman of God Ministry has provided a platform for her to speak, share her poetry, and now as a contributing author to "Picking up the Pieces," Ms. Berry sees this as God's nudge to complete her first book. Her message is "God is real, live authentically with passion, and share your gift of life with others."

Chapter 6

Your Next Assignment Has Already Been Written

In 1996, after being held hostage twice in a three-week period by my estranged husband and him eventually being killed by the local Kansas City police after a five- hour standoff, I struggled with being a statistic of domestic violence and calling myself a Domestic Violence Survivor. Although it was true, I had survived such a traumatic ordeal. I kept asking myself, "Was I really a survivor of domestic violence?" I wasn't getting beaten and physically abused on a regular basis like other women I knew. Yea, my husband and I had arguments throughout our six-year

> *The Lord began showing me that it wasn't the label 'Domestic Violence Survivor' that I was struggling with. I didn't want to accept and/or see the person inside... Me.*

relationship. But we only had three physical fights (one before we got married, one during the marriage which caused us to separate and then the actual hostagesituations). But I struggled with that 'label' for a long time. The Lord began showing me that it wasn't the label 'Domestic Violence Survivor' that I was struggling with. I didn't want to accept and/or see the person inside... Me. I didn't want to deal with the deep-rooted things nor did I know how to deal with the things the Lord was showing and speaking to me. I felt ashamed and guilty. I asked the Lord, "Why are you bringing all this stuff up? It's old, and I can't fix it." It was very painful to look at this grown woman in the mirror and realize I carried deep scars and hurts. Scars I didn't want to acknowledge and some hurts that I didn't even know were there.

Several months after being held hostage twice, things were starting to get back to normal, or should I say, I was getting back to my normal routine of work, church and raising my two children. The physical scars were healing and now I had to focus on healing mentally.

My mother was my biggest support and cheerleader and she often told me, "One day you're going to speak to women all over the world. You're going to be the next Joyce Meyer." I would smile at her because I really didn't see that ever happening, and I even wondered why she kept saying it. But along with her voice in my head, came the stirring in my spirit. I began having dreams and being reminded of dreams from the past of me walking out onto a stage at a very large arena. As these dreams, thoughts and feelings became more frequent, I became confused and wondered what it all meant. I felt scared and unworthy. Who wanted to hear my story? Why would anyone want to hear such a traumatic and dismal story about domestic violence? What made my experience noteworthy of speaking to those that are or have experienced much worse than I did? All these questions constantly ran through my mind.

> "Through your testimony, people will see my Love and begin to see themselves as I see them."

Then the Lord spoke to me and said, "I didn't keep you from dying at the age of twenty-one from a grapefruit size bowel tumor and six blood transfusions in less than twenty-four hours and from two hostage situations just for you to go on living your life as normal." He continued, "When you heard me say, "It's Not Your Time" during that first hostage situation, it's because I've got a plan and something for you to do. You are going to speak to women and share your life story of growing up wanting affection from your father; three broken marriages; low self-esteem and how I brought you out of an abusive situation. Through your testimony, people will see my Love and begin to see themselves as I see them." I was in disbelief and utter amazement at the same time. Wondering how and who would really want to hear my story.

I continued to struggle and the more I resisted, the stronger the voice of the Holy Spirit and the clearer the assignment became. I started to realize that I didn't want to face reality or my truth. Yes, I loved the Lord and I went to church faithfully, but the Lord was showing me how much more growth I needed because He had work for me to do. My next assignment was already written, and the Lord was revealing it to me.

But I had to heal first before I could help anyone else. I had to overcome my fears by first realizing and accepting that I was still alive, not so I could just go on living. Someone else, by hearing my testimony, would see their worth and that they too have a purpose in this world.

This was a big responsibility, but the Holy Spirit kept speaking and reassuring me that He was with me. I started changing my mindset by reaffirming myself. I realized I didn't have to live as a victim. Instead of suppressing all the hurt, I began to deal with it and see who I really was from the inside out. I dealt with the fear and low self-esteem by surrounding myself with family and people that didn't want anything from me but for me to become the best me. I sought counsel from God's Word. And one day, I finally gave my thoughts and feelings a voice. I began to share my testimony with my family and close friends. And I found out, people really did want to not just hear my story, they wanted to know how I got out; how I overcame the fear and why I was not crazy or depressed. I repeatedly heard, "How is it that you still have hope for a good relationship?"

After many more months of wrestling spiritually, I repented and began to accept the path and journey the Lord was taking me on. I constantly prayedand asked for God's wisdom and guidance because I didn't want to make another mistake. I wanted Him to make things clear so I wouldn't get confused trying to accomplish His plan. I'm a very analytical person, and I wanted to see things before I moved. But God was saying, "Janice, that's not how faith works. I want you to trust me with everything in you and move as I direct you."

The Lord told me to go back to the instructions He had given me years ago when I asked whether I should marry my third husband. I grew up in the church and I knew believers weren't supposed to marry unbelievers. But I wanted what I wanted, and I tried to get God to co-sign on my desire. Here's what the Holy Spirit said when I prayed, "This is not who I have for you. But if you choose to marry him, you are going to have to do three things and I'll keep you:

1. Trust Me totally. Stop listening to others and depend totally on Me.

2. Get into your Word daily so you will know and hear the voice of God.

3. Read 1 Corinthians 7:10-16."

Only this time, He reassured me that He was going to be with me throughout this process and told me to meditate on Jeremiah 29:11, "For I know the plans I have for you," declares the LORD, "plans to prosper you and not to harm you, plans to give you hope and a future"(NIV). And as I continued to study the Word of God, I kept being directed to John 14:15, "If you [really] love Me, you will keep (obey) My commands"(AMPC). It's amazing that the Word of God never changes and for me His instructions had not changed. I finally set aside the fear and accepted the assignment the Lord has for me which is to speak to and empower women.

Don't think for one moment that it's been smooth sailing over the years. This journey has been extremely challenging and frustrating at times, but also very rewarding.

Did I know what to do first? Absolutely Not! I didn't know where to start. But I prayed, and the Lord showed me that I had already started on the assignment. I was always sharing my testimony and eventually I penned it and authored my first book, *Torn Between Religion and Relationship*. I was speaking to women and young girls at the jails, conferences, on the radio, workshops, schools, even on TV. I founded a nonprofit organization called Woman of Character, Inc. and continued to speak to businesses and at women's conferences. My book has been scripted for a feature film, and we're looking for investors to help us spread this message of 'hope' and reach the world, so young girls and ladies can avoid unhealthy relationships.

Although I'm not on the stage yet like Joyce Meyer and some days are harder than others because there are so many distractions, I have hope. And, I can still hear my mother's words and continue to feel the stirring of the Holy Spirit to fulfill the plan and purpose set before me to speak to and help women all around this world combat the silent killer known as domestic violence.

> *But I prayed, and the Lord showed me that I had already started on the assignment.*

As the Lord has revealed to me the purpose for my life, I'm encouraging you to ask God to reveal your assignment to you. I guarantee you it's already been written. You just have to ask and accept the call and remember Joshua 1:9, "Have not I commanded you? Be strong, vigorous, and very courageous. Be not afraid, neither be dismayed, for the Lord your God is with you wherever you go" (AMPC).

I won't forget or stop believing in the promises that God has made to me. And you shouldn't either, because God's plan and purpose for your life will happen. Just know that it's a process and what you're going through now is strengthening and preparing you for your next assignment. Stay prayerful and focus on God's promises. And remember, your footsteps have already been ordered by the Lord, just start walking and trust that God's got you. After all, He's the one that has given you the assignment.

In July 1996, **_Janice Butler_** found herself in a horrific situation where her estranged husband held her hostage at gunpoint. Her eventual freedom came after a five hour standoff,

which resulted in him being fatally shot and killed by Kansas City police officers. Janice Butler is now an author, speaker and the founder of Woman of Character, Inc., which is a Missouri based non-profit Domestic Violence 501(c)(3) organization. As a speaker and the author of "Torn between Religion and Relationship", Janice empowers women by sharing her own personal experience with domestic violence and self-esteem issues and encourages women and young ladies across the nation to see themselves as God sees them and to realize their own "value" and "self- worth". Janice is committed to providing education and resource information on domestic violence and the cycle of abuse so that women are better informed and will ultimately have the knowledge to make better decisions and choices about their relationships.

Janice has served as a church leader, women's ministry director, and teacher. She is the proud mother of two adult children and three grandchildren. Janice is passionate about uplifting others through her testimony and God given abilities.

Chapter 7

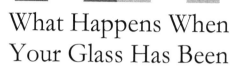

What Happens When Your Glass Has Been

Have you ever dropped a plate on the ground leaving behind shards of sharp pieces of glass? After you dropped the plate, did you leave it there for someone else to step on and possibly cut themselves? Or did you clean it up yourself? Picking up the pieces can hurt and sometimes, you might even cut yourself in the process of cleaning it up. But, somebody has to do it. Who better than you?

Picture, if you will, one of those fancy looking vases made up of a billion pieces of broken glass – a mosaic vase. From something broken, an artisan renders a beautiful work of art. This is the story of what happened when my glass shattered.

As a child, I didn't have much to worry about. My family was (appeared) ideal. My mom didn't work. She was a stay at home mom who occasionally turned our home into a baby-sitting service, "watching" my cousins and me. My dad was a police officer who left in the morning to go to work and returned home just in time for dinner. He was super laid back and chill. As soon as he came home, he'd change into his night clothes and turn on Sanford and Son or a good old western movie.

> I remember looking at him and trying to force myself to cry because I thought I should cry too.

Up until I was in the first grade, my family remained put together. We weren't the richest family, but we weren't dead broke. If we were, my parents did a good job at hiding it...kind of. In school, I received reduced and then free lunch. And even though I was young, I knew what that meant. Our family funds were lower. I remember coming home from school one day, and my mom sat my brother and I down at the kitchen table. She broke the news that we were moving. I don't know what made me ask, but I asked Mom if Dad was coming with us. She answered no, and my brother broke out in tears. I remember looking at him and trying to force myself to cry because I thought I should cry too.

When my parents first separated, I didn't really understand it. In all honesty, at first I thought it was cool to have two homes, two different lifestyles, and two different sets of friends depending on who's house I was at. But, that got old quick. At Mom's house, all we ever had to eat were grilled cheese sandwiches. She had this triangle sandwich maker thing, and for some reason that was dinner almost every day. At Dad's house, all he ever had was candy, Rolo's, popcorn, and hotdogs. I might have only been seven years old, but I remember those details vividly. I loved going to see Dad but hated leaving because I always cried. It got to the point where I didn't want to go see my dad because I knew I would cry when Mom came to get us. Looking back on it now, I wish I would have spent more time at my Dad's house.

> *I finally had my own bedroom. My life was perfect... (Temporarily perfect).*

Thankfully, my parents were only separated for about two years. God works in mysterious ways, and He must have known I needed both of my parents in my life equally because He blessed my family and allowed my parents to get back together. We were a family again AND my dad had been promoted in the police department which meant more money and a bigger house. In the third grade, my family moved out of the hood and into the suburbs. I finally had my own bedroom. My life was perfect... (Temporarily perfect).

"Perfect" didn't last long, four years to be exact. On December 22, 2007, my glass was shattered into a gazillion and one pieces. A thirteen- year-old girl, a real daddy's girl was now left fatherless. Almost ten years later, and I still remember it like yesterday. The day before it happened, my best friend had invited me to her family's Christmas party.

I went into my parent's room and asked my dad if I could go with her. Of course, he told his *Pooh* yes. "Pooh", that's the nickname he'd given me.

I never thought that would be the last time I talked to my dad. Our last conversation consisted of him laughing at some ridiculous thing I said. I probably asked for some money, knowing me. And it ended with a kiss and a whisper from him saying, "Be good." I left home and that was the last time I would ever see my dad alive. The next day, my older sister was supposed to take me to the mall so I could finish my Christmas shopping, but that didn't happen... I awoke to the doorbell constantly ringing.

Before I could make it downstairs, my sister brought me into her room and uttered the words, "Mom and Dad were in a car accident...and Daddy didn't make it." Remember those shards of sharp glass I spoke of earlier? Those pieces were all over my sister's room and remained in her room for years. A rush of emotions hit me all at once. I fell back onto my sister's bed and cried profusely. I remember going into the bathroom and dialing my dad's cell phone number hoping that he would answer. The phone went straight to voicemail over and over and over again. A new chapter in my life was about to begin...a chapter without Dad. I knew God was real. My mom took us to church. I was an acolyte. I said my blessing before I ate dinner. I did that stuff. But what kind of God would take a child's father away? A good man away from the world, at that. I began to question God's love for me because it just was not fair.

I did a pretty good job at pretending to be "okay." Stay away from your family, fake a smile, don't cry out loud, and follow the number one rule: Don't let anyone ask you if you are okay. Avoid that question at all cost! We all know we can fake happy, but as soon as someone asks, "Are you okay," the water works come. It gets me every time, even now.

My mom decided to make us go to grief counseling, which I thought was a waste of time and the dumbest thing ever. I didn't tell her that. But in my head, that's what I was thinking. We only went to two sessions, and I was happy about that. I didn't like to hear people, let alone a pastor tell me, "He's with God...You'll see him again...It's a time for everything." For the sake of this book, I'll just say I thought everything people were telling me was straight up "crap." I didn't care what anybody had to say about God because my God wouldn't cause such confusion and hurt, right? Wrong.

I am not the type of person to talk about my feelings, especially when I'm sad. In full disclosure, I've only recently became comfortable saying the word sad because for so long I associated sadness with weakness, and I didn't like to feel weak. To avoid talking to people I wrote in a notebook.

One day, my mom and I got into it, and I went upstairs to my bedroom and wrote a prayer asking God to take me up to Heaven to be with my dad. Yep, essentially, I wanted to die too. I wasn't going to go to any extreme and kill myself, but I had it in my head that I needed to be in Heaven with my dad because that was where I belonged. I was just a teenager, about sixteen or seventeen years old when I wrote that note. The next day I went to the cemetery where my dad was buried. I hardly ever went there, but something kept telling me to go so I did. When I got there, anger filled my heart. I was mad at everything and to top it off, I couldn't find his gravesite. Like I said before, I rarely visited the cemetery so it was all confusing to me, and I did not want to have to call my Mom and tell her I was lost. I didn't want anyone to know where I was or what I was doing. After walking circles in the cold, I finally made my way to the front office where they gave me a map which directed me to his gravesite. I'm not sure why I didn't think to go to the front office when I arrived, but when I finally got there and arrived at his gravesite, all the anger instantly left my body, instantly. I began to cry, not just the "I'm frustrated cry," but the kind of cry you do when you've been holding so much in for years and you just need to release it all.

Five years of holding in the pain of losing my father came out within minutes. For the first time, I felt God wrap His arms around me, and I knew for myself God was real. In the midst of my tears, I asked God why. I can't say I received an answer, but I can say I received the reassurance I needed. All the years prior, I knew God was real, but I had never felt Him until that moment. If a stranger saw me, they probably thought I was the crazy by the way I was having a full on conversation with my dad's spirit and God. I left the cemetery that day feeling refreshed and at peace. I had never experienced a feeling like that and to experience God with my dad was amazing. My dad wasn't one to go to church, but he knew his Bible, and he definitely instilled in his children that God was real. My dad would buy the monthly Daily Breads, and I remember reading one with him and signing the back confessing my faith and declaring that God would have a seat for me in Heaven when I got there. When I look back on it that is probably one of the best memories I have with my dad, experiencing God...with him.

It's safe to say I am that mosaic vase. When my sister told me that my Dad had passed away, I broke. And, I remained broken for years, but the beauty of a mosaic vase cannot be seen without something breaking. Those broken shards of glass that sometimes hurt when you pick them up are my testimonies and the challenges I face. In my life, I know there are going to be many more times I have to pick up shards of broken glass and make it part of my masterpiece. I challenge you to remember that even when you are at your lowest point in life, you don't have to remain a broken piece of glass waiting to hurt someone else. Pick up the broken pieces yourself and turn it into a masterpiece. Be your own mosaic vase and let your beauty of your brokenness shine through.

Andrea Alexis Chism is a native of Kansas City, MO and now resides in Dallas, Texas with her dog "FAITH". Andrea is a graduate of the University

of North Texas with a Bachelor of Science Degree in Kinesiology, which is the study of human and non-human movement of the body. Andrea had the honor of being crowned as the 2012 Miss Debutante.

Andrea loves playing piano, baking, dancing and spending time with friends and family. She believes that every shattered piece of glass fits perfectly into your very own Masterpiece.

Chapter 8

Love Struck

I must admit that I have some beautiful girlfriends who have been long term friends, some as far back as childhood. Although I kept my unhappy marriage a secret for a long time, I started to open up once I pursued a divorce.

I felt like I had been cheated out of true love during my marriage.

One of my girlfriends took me out to happy hour, and we met a group of guys. We laughed, talked and drank. It was fun. There was one guy I was interested in. Unfortunately, I found out weeks later he wasn't interested in me. Disappointed, I decided happy hour was not my cup of tea. Afterwards, another friend suggested I try online dating.

"Oh, NO WAY!" I exclaimed vehemently. I knew many people met that way, and that it was the new way to date, but I didn't want any part of it. Many weeks went by, and I dropped into a spiral of depression. Yearning for love, I grew sadder. I felt like I had been cheated out of true love during my marriage and I wanted to experience it in this lifetime. I wanted a companion, a soul mate. I had so much love built up inside, and I wanted to put these emotions to good use on a deserving man.

"Why not go ahead and try this online dating?" I said to myself. I ran upstairs, jumped on my computer and signed up. Within fifteen minutes, I was online.

"WOW... I did it. I can't believe it," I whispered to myself, not knowing my life had just changed forever. My desire to love someone and to have someone love me back was so strong that I would do almost anything, and that is what I did.

Almost immediately, I met someone online. His picture was gorgeous, and his profile made me dream of someone else being out there who wanted the same things I did. I reached out to him, and he responded. He said all the right things and showed me attention like I had never experienced before. I fell for him almost right away, and we hadn't even met in person. Our relationship was wonderful, and I enjoyed our talks on the phone and online.

He often talked about plans to marry one day and buying a big house together. I loved those talks because it made me seem loved. Not knowing I was being set up for a plot that was brewing. This man was out of town most of our relationship. He claimed he had business in other countries he needed to attend to. It bothered me because I wanted to meet him in person. I wanted us to hold each other, kiss each other, and take long walks in the park together. Every time I asked when we could see each other he would say as soon as he returned to the U.S. I was a patient woman. I believed love was worth waiting for.

After several months of this, I started to pull away because the relationship was draining me.

The longer he stayed overseas, the more trouble happened to him. Then, his trouble started to affect me financially and emotionally. He took me through some trying times, and he always had these unbelievably sob stories. My longing for true love made me feel close to him at times and yet so far. He knew how much of a hopeless romantic I was, and he used that in his favor.

After several months of this, I started to pull away because the relationship was draining me. When he noticed I wasn't as interested as I used to be, he pulled another ploy to get me back under his wing.

One day, I arrived home to flowers, a teddy bear and a box of candy. I jumped for joy. I brought the gifts inside and admired how beautiful everything was. I felt like I was the envy of all women. The card read, "I love you and miss you." It touched my heart so much, I was back under his spell again. I called him to thank him for the gifts, and he was excited I had received them.

Over the next few days, I noticed a police car parked periodically across the street from my house. I didn't pay much attention to it. I had never been in trouble with the law, not even as much as a speeding ticket. The next day, the same thing happened. Again, the police car was parked outside my house. The next day I came home and there was a business card in my door from a detective. He asked me to call him. I started to worry. Why would a detective want to talk to me?

All that night and into the morning, I worried about what the police wanted with me. Then it dawned on me, I bet this online man I was talking to was behind this. I called him repeatedly, but he did not answer. I emailed him over and over again. Still, no reply. Now I knew something was wrong.

The next day I went to the detective's office, and he put me in an interrogation room and locked the door. I couldn't believe what was happening to me. All I wanted was to love someone and have them love me back. I was not a criminal. And yet, I was being accused of criminal activity I had no idea I was involved in. I explained to the officer that I started talking to a man I met on the internet, but I had never seen him physically. The detective explained to me that the man was a scammer. My heart sunk to the deepest low. I couldn't believe I had allowed someone to scam me. All I wanted was someone to love.

As the weeks and months went by, I experienced a wave of emotions. Deep depression, sadness, hatred, bitterness, self-pity, closed heartedness and forgiveness. Yes, forgiveness. I had made a mess of my life all in the name of LOVE. I was enraptured by the imagery of being with my soul mate and lost hold of good common sense.

As time passed, my depression diminished, and I had no choice but to pick up the pieces and get my life on track again. But how would I piece my life back together? I reflected on what happened and why. The most hurtful part was my dream of being in love was over. I tried to pray to get some type of answer as to why this happened to me, but I felt like God wasn't hearing me. I was embarrassed and didn't want to see a psychologist. I was a different person now, one I didn't like.

After a few years of tears and self-destruction, I decided to put everything into perspective. First, I had to identify the issue I was having within myself.

I was a hopeless romantic and realized I had never received love from a man ever in my life. I wanted to love someone and have someone love me unconditionally. I realized I didn't have the strength to love myself, so I relied on a man to give me what I needed... LOVE.

Second, I had to admit the real issue. I had low self- esteem. I admit, I wanted love so badly that I would accept almost anything a man told me in the name of love. I admit, I can be gullible. I admit, I have a big heart, and I always want to help others in need. This trait of mine is obvious, and people have been known to use it in their favor. I admit that often times I second guess myself in situations I know aren't right, but I justify my actions in hopes of being in love. I admit, I settle for crumbs from a man when I deserve the cake.

Third, I had to heal. This was the most important step. To heal, I had to identify and then admit the real issue. If I was stuck on step two and in denial, step three the healing process couldn't happen. I blamed the man for all the evil things he did to me. It seemed like the easiest answer, but I was wrong. Blaming him did give me some peace, but it didn't completely heal me. In fact, blaming him only made me blame myself more.

I wanted to heal. I wanted to break free from the misery. Since the scammer was not a real person, I had no one to release my anger on except me. I needed to heal from within and rid myself of this heartache forever. So, I asked myself, how could I love myself all by myself? I started a daily routine of waking up each morning, looking in the mirror without any makeup on, messed up hair and teeth unbrushed, and saying to myself, "You are a beautiful woman and God loves you." I repeated that affirmation several times each morning. And I continued to repeat it until it became my truth.

I had to forgive. Yes, I said it, forgive the evil scammer. I admit, that was a tough one. I was so angry at this faceless person that forgiving him was extremely hard to do. To forgive him, I had to think that maybe he too had low self-esteem. He probably thought people owed him money, and he would take it by any means necessary.

I had to forgive myself. I tapped into who I truly am as a person and how God made me. God made me loving, caring, thoughtful, humble, and understanding, a helper to those in need.

> *I was able to forgive him after I forgave myself.*

The scammer was a troubled human being. Years later, I actually felt sorry for him. I was able to forgive him after I forgave myself. I realized that I was trying to help someone whom I thought was truly in need. For that, I am proud because that is my mission on this earth.

Unfortunately, I used my self-worth on the wrong person. Nevertheless, I acted as God would want me to act. The lesson I learned is to pick and choose when and who I help. I don't want to change the core of my being because someone used me. I have learned my lesson, and I refuse to let this happen to me again.

Part of my healing process was to sit quietly and reflect. I took time away from men and sat and thought about myself. I realized I had to stop being so needy for love. God knows my heart. I don't have to worry about trying to find my soul mate. God has him already in mind for me. All I need is to wait on him and have faith that He will give me the desires of my heart.

My desire now is to tell my story to prevent others from falling in the same trap I did. Believe in God first and ask Him for the desires of your heart, then sit back and watch God work.

Andrea Larbi was born in northern part of the United States; currently residing in the south. Without having siblings as a child, she had to be very creative in her play and thinking. In her early 30's, she wrote a blog about her trip to China. It was seen all over the world.

Andrea was complimented on her writing style and told how people felt as though they were living the same adventure through her words. A "little birdie" told her to *officially* write a book. Andrea has spent many years thinking of what to say or share in a book as her calling has been to help others. Then it hit her! As a self-proclaimed hopeless romantic; always searching for that one true love, her soul mate. Andrea realized that she was not the only one who feels this way. Over the course of her lifetime, this passion for finding her one true love had taken her down some dark and slippery roads.

Andrea is pleased and grateful to co-author, "Picking up the Pieces". In the near future, you will find more books from her on romance, love and heart break. All with a single message of regaining your sense of one-ness with GOD as He designed you. Love yourself as GOD loves you even more.

Chapter 9

Tell It Until You're Heard

Thinking back to my earlier years as a young girl I had struggled with being heard by others, including by my siblings, or at least in my mind I had thought this was the case. I clearly had some traits I struggled with expressing my feelings since it seemed that when I tried, it appeared I was speaking a foreign language that no one could understand. Or my words were misconstrued and caused dissent within my family circle. Before I knew it my behavior of being silent and feeling left out

> *Daily, I popped the pills without a thought as one would take their own one a day vitamin to promote good health.*

had been carried over into my adult life, therefore, when my psychiatrist years later diagnosed me with bipolar disease, although I was not certain, I accepted the label. Not that I was excited about being diagnosed with a psychological disorder, but it would explain my ongoing battle with myself and the feelings of being misplaced in the world. After years of being analyzed, finally I was given a medical diagnosis which came with a long tumultuous journey of taking multiple prescription medications. However, the pills prescribed never seemed to work unless I over indulged with the use of alcohol. By mixing the two I knew that it was a recipe for disaster, yet I was desperate to calm the anxiety and attain some sort of normalcy. I was willing to do what it took to get me there. It was the one thing that could buffer the pain that I had lived with for much too long because of the many skeletons in my past. Remember, I am the middle child, so forgive me if it seems like I am slow to tell my story.

Over the next several years, I faithfully took the medication that was promised to temper my symptoms of the mental illness. Daily, I popped the pills without a thought as one would take their own one a day vitamin to promote good health. Unbeknownst to me, and apparently to my prescribing physicians, the medication was doing quite the opposite; harming me physically and emotionally. When I finally disclosed to my sisters that I had been diagnosed with bipolar disorder, it gave me hope that I could move forward with my life, especially since I thought I knew what I was dealing with and I had the support and love from my family. But as time passed, I became frustrated and instead of seeing the light at the end of the pills I was ordered to take, I began to see only darkness with intermittent depression always looming close by. Although my income wasn't substantial it was steady, and I took pride in staying on top of my bills and handling my financial affairs, so when the doctor bills began to pile up, it exasperated my already declining mental state. I often asked myself, "Does anybody care, and why are they not listening to me?" I recall one of my sisters saying, "You are not bipolar and stop claiming everything people put on you."

But no longer will I blame myself.

She was my voice echoing what my mind was thinking. If only I was courageous enough to communicate with the doctors all of the missing information that could have helped them in properly diagnosing me, I could have been spared much of the grief and undue stress that I went through. From the first day I stepped into my doctor's office, I subconsciously left out very important information about my past. At the time I do not think that I intentionally left it out, but I was young and did not understand the importance of sharing all the gory details. Now that I look back, it was detrimental to my mental recovery. If

I were to be honest, withholding the vital information about my past was more about me not wanting to be judged, and I was embarrassed about my questionable life choices. There were times I wanted to point fingers and blame my doctors for the misdiagnoses, but because of my fear in telling the story of what happened to me I was hugely at fault. Understandably so, since I believe many in my shoes would probably choose to keep a tight lid on being victimized believing the lie that the blame falls on their shoulder. But no longer will I blame myself. Years earlier I had experienced a traumatic experience that had seriously affected me however, that is another chapter within itself..

If you weren't studying me too closely, you might think that I was a person of confidence as I walked quickly, with my head held high and singing my favorite two-word phrase when asked how I was. "I'm fine, I'm fine." But let the truth be told, after the many years past I was still trying to find a voice to speak up and be heard so I could get the help I desperately needed. When the doctor diagnosed me with bipolar disease it was like a great escape for me to get as far away as possible from the truth that had traumatized me. Looking back, I see how it gave me an excuse to not talk about my dark past. I could put it away, pretending it was just a nightmare and over time it would slip away from my memory. Being diagnosed with bipolar disorder in my mind gave me a pass and I foolishly thought I would be able to conceal my emotions and re-event myself, I was ever so wrong. By accepting the diagnosis, it had caused me more grief. With the acceptance, I became more anxious, paranoid, and I rarely was honest with my family and friends. I began to overmedicate, which caused me to be admitted into the hospital a few times. I knew if I was going to get the help from my doctors, and calm the confusion and the chatter of my inner voice I would need to face my demons and talk about my past.

I began the practice of using my outer voice as I engaged in conversations with God. Those spiritual two- way conversations led me to church, where I eventually joined and became a regular attendee. When I say there are angels on earth, believe me. The human angels I met there were instrumental in helping me feel safe and comfortable with talking about my painful, dark past.

Because I was well groomed on the outside and seemed to have it together many found it difficult to believe me when I confessed that for years I've battled with a dark secret. Finally, the young girl trapped inside of me had cried out for help from my doctor. I told him about my traumatic experience that I had endured many years ago. When he said the words, "You do not have bipolar disorder. You have Post Traumatic Stress Syndrome brought on by your painful past". That remark, resonated over and over! The abuse wasn't my fault. Being kidnapped wasn't my fault. It wasn't my FAULT!! I said it loud and clear.

At times I have thought back to if only I could had found the courage to speak up and loud enough so I could be heard. The progression of healing could have started much sooner. However, I am reminded to be forgiving and gentle to my younger self, knowing that I only did what I could do at the time. The attempt was not to hurt myself but to protect my wounded self in any way possible. Therefore I chose silence, until I was ready to speak my truth. Today I feel as if the weight of the world has been lifted off my shoulders, and I pray that whoever reads my story, that it may encourage you to speak up as soon as you can so that you too may be put on your journey to healing much sooner than me. I realize I have a voice, and for me to move forward, I must speak it until I am heard. I am shouting it out from the top of my lungs "Tell It Until You Are Heard" because if you keep quiet or don't speak loud enough, life will continue to move on, as you continue to half live. Believe in yourself and know that it is your responsibility to be heard so that you may heal.

Tina Marie Berry- Pescatori is a native of Kansas City, Missouri currently residing in Las Vegas Nevada with her fur baby, "Ms. Bruno". She has worked in the optical field over 27 years. When Tina isn't working, her time is spent praying, helping and doing what she can to serve others. She loves her church family.

She is a member of Nehemiah Ministries, where she serves with the Chosen Woman Ministry. Tina enjoys, running and working out!

Chapter 10

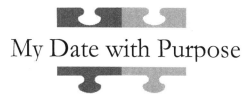

My Date with Purpose

There she is still sitting on the bench just waiting her turn to share. The lady before her had two things she said that resonated, but she couldn't help but feel like there was something left unsaid. She was holding it in, almost like holding her breath. She started, but she hadn't hit the crux of what had been troubling this feisty crowd. These women who were sitting there just waiting to release. You know the types, the ones who need encouragement from someone outside their hometown because inside they're left out. The ones who hold signs that say, "Will travel for inspiration", these signs written on their hearts instead of cardboard. Still, the ones who have been waiting for those closest to them to see them, but who never even get a second glance.

In fact, it's me. I'm waiting, waiting for her to tell me it's okay to let it out. The one with a voice that doesn't get raised. The one who runs rings around most, but constantly takes jabs from those who only wish they had a portion of the confidence. Yet, I'm still waiting. Just waiting. Patiently waiting. Finally, the lady comes from off the stage and as she comes toward the bench, she looks at me while tossing her hair and says

to me, "They're ready for you." I couldn't believe it. I turned around, looking behind me. She had to be talking to someone else or at least maybe for that moment, I was hoping she was. The director called for me. He said, "They're about to introduce you." Now, it's fade to black and I'm waiting for them to say my name. My moment was before me, and I had been waiting on it all my life. I could hear the song. Phil Collins was singing, and it was just about the time for the drums to kick in on the hook, and he said, "The lady you've been waiting for all night. She's about to hit the stage. The wait is over. Stand to your feet and help me welcome to the Madison Square Garden..."

> *For the past month, I've had the same dream. I'm waiting, then it's my turn and I wake up.*

Then I woke up. I opened my eyes and looked at the calendar, but couldn't make out the date. Where were my glasses? For the past month,

I've had the same dream. I'm waiting, then it's my turn and I wake up. Over the past few years, I'd been doing everything I could to run my business and work my nine to five. I have a boss, but then I am a boss too. It's the double life of a B5. You know the term right, B5? It's the B for business owner, but also working a nine to five, B5. If you hadn't heard that before, it's okay. I've now coined the phrase. I had been working to build a publishing company for the past two years. I started out with my own book and it wasn't quite what I had envisioned, so I endeavored to make it better for others who were like me. Just starting out, but wanting a product that looked like I'd been doing this for years. I've always been like that. I wanted to look like I'd done it before, even if I hadn't. I wanted to not just appear like a pro, but become the pro in the process. I was never afraid of process, but I was afraid of where the process would take me. Though, I was more of afraid of staying still if I didn't allow the process to get me where God wanted me to go.

I don't have the story of tragedy to triumph. My testimony has been that I just worked on it, little by little, then it grew. On the inside of me was an ever- burning desire to be greater than what I was. I believe that God had infused me with being part woman and part angel at the same time. You see, I help people become who God has created them to be. He gives me ideas, formulas, systems, thoughts, words and wisdom for other people. I have seen many take something I gave them and turn it into their million-dollar baby. I mean that, literally. I had a friend who, with just a quick tagline I shared with him for his product, has gone on to sell one item to over a million households in America alone. He calls me every now and then to ask me how things are going and to tell me he appreciates how I helped him launch. Every time I take his call, I ask God, "God, when am I going to launch? Do I have an angel there for me?" Now, I can't say he has never sent me a gift to express thanks or just left me hanging.

He hasn't. He sends us a card every year. But the reality is when we were chatting and coming up with ideas, he wasn't my client. He doesn't owe me anything but gratitude for helping him define or tag his product. I owed him a thank you too. It was because of him I realized there was purpose alive and well in me. I know there is something within me that is just waiting for my launch. It's a set time; a date with purpose. It's the date that God gave me to be released into purpose. But the date hadn't been determined. He knew when it would be. I just didn't know.

I'm awake now. I haven't had that dream in a few years. I'm in traffic trying to move through the hustle and bustle of holiday shoppers, workers heading home and city buses moving people from place to place. I'm driving down the main drag of the inner city looking around at everything I left behind. We moved to the suburbs and the city sees me now very infrequently. But the lights, the action, the brisk air across my chilled nose reminds me of my days walking to the Plaza to see the lights come on, on Thanksgiving. I rolled down the window to take a sniff of the chilly air and see if I could catch the smell of Topsy's popcorn, KC Masterpiece BBQ or even the yucky smell of horses pulling couples

She filled my cup with royal nuggets that seemed straight from the throne room.

in carriages. I've been a dreamer all my life. I've written many pages of what my life was going to be like, and sometimes I still try to remember stories that were left untold. The ones I started on pages of my steno notebook or the pink three ring Trapper Keeper binder I had in 10th grade. They were my stories; brief flights of life for the heroines and the villains. The emerging business woman or the eccentric Renaissance man.

They were many and they were mine. As I roll up the car window, it reminds me that I've not yet rolled up into my dreams. I'm still working on them. Every day is yet another day closer to the purpose He planned just for me. My date was undetermined, but my purpose wasn't.

It's been more than five years now, and I'm unsure of exactly what it is they're asking of me. I've been sitting here waiting. I wanted to go first and start the dominoes falling, but I was asked to finish it up and close out the evening instead. It was fine. I tell my children to set the tone and be the example, so whenever I have the chance I like to do that too, literally. The woman who was originally invited to be the evening speaker had turned ill and couldn't make it. So, I was asked to fill in at the last minute. "Sure," I said, "what time should I get there?" At around six thirty, I could see the crowd growing tired. They were yawning, and the weariness of the day began to illuminate the room. I just settled in and grasped the truths being told by the lady who went before me. She was scholarly and filled with wisdom. I hadn't heard anyone like this in a while. She filled my cup with royal nuggets that seemed

> *Today, your purpose is meeting you right here.*

straight from the throne room. My cup was running over. If nothing else, this was a good night for me. My eyes were closed as I enjoyed the sounds of the Word from heaven and the melodious woman soloist. It was good for me to be in the house. The next thing I know, I hear the woman with a microphone say, "Well, your wait is over. Stand to your feet and help me welcome Michelle Gines to Madison Square." Now, I was awake.

Eyes wide open and tears rolling down my face, I made my way to the front of the platform and lifted my hands. Seeing this once weary room on their feet — awaiting their time of release, I spoke to the room. "Who's waiting for you? Who's needing a glance from your eyes in affirmation?

Whose encouragement are you holding in?" I asked again and again. "What are you waiting for? Who are you waiting on? Today is your day. Today is the date. Today, your purpose is meeting you right here." It was my date too. I could feel the heartbeat of every woman there who needed permission to speak up. The ones who came to be seen. Not for what they're wearing, but for what they've been trying to say. Release and Results are all a part of the exhale of the journey.

I began to share the story of being young and singing in front of Grandma's mirror on the bathroom

wall. The created stories in my mind that lived inside me to be told outside of my human walls. They could hear me. I knew because they responded. With each question, there were women who received. They had been waiting. Patiently waiting. This was their date and mine. As women, we sometimes have limited our lives to only what we can get a view of in magazines, often not feeling like it could be me. But the truth is when it's your time, God will send an angel to speak to you just like He did for Mary, Hannah and Sarai. The date isn't always a date that can be circled with a red marker on a calendar page, but often it comes when you least expect it. It comes when you're not looking for it, but when your heart is ready for it. It's your release!

If you blow up a balloon but don't tie it shut, when you release it and let go, everything on the inside of that balloon fills the atmosphere. But even with balloons, because they look pretty blown up, we try to leave them up as long as possible. People aren't balloons. People can't hold their breath that long. People need to be released. You need to be released. Your date, your release into your purpose— stop holding it in. Let it out.

People need to hear it. People need to hear you. Speak. Share. Release. I waited, and the waiting gave me an expectation. When it was time, the date

was marked, and I took center stage, for them and for me. I'm here to encourage you to be ready for your release. It's coming. You too have a date with purpose.

Who says that "Intention is the only way that works"? ***Michelle Gines.*** Why, because only what we intend to do gets done. As a publisher, author and speaker, Michelle Gines, spends a lot of time with people. People who make plans. People who follow through on plans. People with no plans and plans that are just waiting for intentional people. That's the sweet spot! Intentional people + Intentional plans = Intended Results.

Michelle served as assistant editor for her high school newspaper and went on to study mass communications in college. Always a passionate reader and storyteller herself, it makes total sense that Michelle now serves as CEO for Purpose

Publishing, a publisher and consulting firm. Grateful now for the encouragement from family and friends, she established the company in 2010 and this year marks the milestone of publishing 100 Books and 100 authors. They ask, how she does it. She answers, with intention. Michelle serves alongside her husband, Minister Brian Gines and their 3 teenage children; Zerryn, Brielle and Charis.

Chapter 11

Life After Death

My Journey from Broken to Whole Again

> The medical definition of <u>Grief:</u> *The normal process of reacting to a loss. The loss may be physical (such as a death), social (such as divorce), or occupational (such as a job). Emotional reactions of grief can include anger, guilt, anxiety, sadness, and despair. Physical reactions of grief can include sleeping problems, changes in appetite, physical problems, or illness.*

There was a time not too long ago I fit that medical definition of grief and I experienced most, if not all, of the emotional and physical reactions noted.

Between February 2013 and October 2015 I lost both parents and my younger sister "Cookie". It felt like before I could get through the stages of grief on one loss another followed. My mother's death came first, I was devastated when she passed. Afterward, I dreamed about her nightly but could never see her face in those dreams. I could only hear her voice or her back would be turned to me. I kept most of what I was going through to myself because it felt like everyone else was doing okay and moving on but I didn't feel like moving on, laughing or enjoying myself because the hurt was too deep. I'm sure in medical books this was not a healthy course to take. I finally asked my father why I never saw my mom's face in

> *I still felt the same but was this a message from God that it was now time for me to move on from this?*

my dreams. He told me when I was ready to accept that she was gone I would see her face again. We talked a lot during that time – he would call me often and I him. One of my sisters got married during this time and I got to see him dancing and having a good time at the wedding. What a glorious day! Seeing him let go of his grief for a few hours made me feel a little better in that moment. It took nearly two years but I finally began to see my mom's face in my dreams. Was I finally accepting her death? Unfortunately within those two years my dad passed before I could share with him that he was right. I still felt the same but was this a message from God that it was now time for me to move on from this? The dreams of my mom became less and farther apart but I saw her face every time. In January 2014 my father passed. Unlike my mother, who had been in ICU for several days prior to going to inpatient hospice, he died suddenly within hours of being rushed to the hospital before I could get a flight to Atlanta. With my mother I was able to be there and enjoy her touch for about two weeks, talk with her and tell her how much I loved her. When the decision was made to discuss end of life options I couldn't do it. My sisters and my niece had to take on that role. I didn't have the strength or courage to hear her last wishes. I felt like such a failure. I'm the oldest but couldn't uphold my responsibility. She had given my niece, a registered nurse, and myself the medical power of attorney, and we both had to sign the DNR paper. I couldn't at first because I felt I would be contributing to her death. I know that may sound strange but it tore me up inside. I prayed I was doing the right thing and signed the paper. Does one ever really know? The grief of my dad's death compounded the grief I was already experiencing from my mother's death.

A few months before my dad died my sister was diagnosed with leiomyosarcoma of the uterus. A very bad prognosis but I thought she's a fifteen year breast cancer survivor, she's going to be okay. After having three surgeries and almost dying on the operating table with her last surgery, she proved it wasn't her time yet even though the doctors didn't expect her to survive the weekend. She was so unbelievably strong, even with this third surgery she was eventually able to walk around the unit. After going to rehab she started declining quickly. I knew this wasn't good and lashed out at the nurses. One day I had a melt down on the unit and went off on everyone; doctors, nurses and therapists. No one was free from the "wrath of Debbie". I knew it wasn't their fault, but I couldn't stop myself, I had to relieve myself of the pain and blame someone. At that point, I knew she was dying and couldn't accept it. I was mad at God...three loved ones in a row. And all these mean, selfish, evil people going on about their business without a care for anyone or anything, prosperous and healthy...I WAS very ANGRY! I found out from my brother-in-law my sister had signed a DNR and would be going home on hospice. She never told me. I assume because she knew I would be emotional. I went to the hospital that afternoon and she asked me not to be mad at her for not telling me about the DNR. I was able to get out that I wasn't mad at her but mad at the situation.

My sister was on hospice care about two weeks prior to passing and in one of her lucid moments she told me "You're the best sister anyone could ask for". This brought tears to my eyes. It was an uplifting moment for me and I cherish that memory to this day.

All of a sudden, she opened her eyes and said "I'm not suffering". Then, she closed her eyes again and didn't wake for several hours.

One day I thought she was sleeping and as I sat in a chair by her bed praying aloud to God, I asked him "not to let my sister suffer". All of a sudden, she opened her eyes and said "I'm not suffering". Then, she closed her eyes again and didn't wake for several hours. I felt that God had heard my plea. Several days after her funeral, a profound wave of loneliness came over me and I didn't know how to handle it. I've been alone but I've never felt lonely. I missed her greatly and cried all the time, while driving, working, walking in the grocery store or even while reading a book...basically at any given moment. To keep my mind occupied and to help with the anger and despair I took Zumba, Tai Chi, guitar lessons, a fitness class, ceramic &

crochet classes. I think you get the idea, whatever it took to drown my thoughts. I wasn't good at any of those things but I kept going and doing my best. I think keeping busy was a must for me to cope during that time. Living with the loss of three cherished loved ones within such a short time frame is overwhelming and truth be told I didn't think I would ever feel like myself again.

> One of the hardest things about living with grief is keeping it inside.

One of the hardest things about living with grief is keeping it inside. I didn't want to bring other people down by mentioning or talking about what I was going through. I tried with a couple family members but they didn't seem to want to have this conversation. Basically, I just wanted an ear to vent to and I figured no one was interested. Or, that I would only make them sad or feel bad and bring their spirits down so I chose not to burden others. I isolated myself from friends and family because it was hard to hide my sadness and I felt better being by myself. I canceled a couple of planned trips because I just couldn't pretend to be happy around people when I was dying inside.

I admit it. I was broken. I remember reading somewhere about how there is a window in your heart and that when the window is cracked by a pebble such as pain, the result is a shattered window. It is hard to see God through a cracked window. He was distorted. It is hard to see Him through the pain and you question why God would let something like this happen. This was such a significant analogy to me. God hadn't left me I just couldn't perceive Him clearly through the pain. This helped me on my road back. What I know for sure is that there is "life after death". In time the darkness will lift. Just know that God will always be beside you and will lead you back to the light. It may not be as quickly as you want but in His time. This timeframe differs for everyone. It may not be easy to get there and I'm not fully there yet myself but I'm getting closer day by day. With good friends, family and faith, I'm comfortable being around people again. I can laugh, joke and interact. I eventually shared what I was feeling and experiencing with several people. With many tears I was able to express what I was going through to some coherent extent. It felt so good to finally purge myself and realize my family, friends and God do care.

I'm feeling 3/4 whole again, I can't admit to being 100% at this time, at least not yet. I've had momentary setbacks but I continue to keep my head up while moving forward. I'll be there soon. Never hold back telling someone you love them. Don't put it off. Share with God your grief and ask for His help when needed. The same goes for family and friends - open up to them about your feelings. Don't try to go it alone.

There is a little book by Lance Wubbels entitled "If Only I Knew". One passage reads "If only I knew that even when everything in my life seems to go wrong and comes crumbling down around me, even when my heart is broken, God has promised to always be with me".

Deborah Jean Jackson Williams is a former resident and native of Kansas City, Missouri; graduating from Southeast High School. Deborah currently works in Health Information Management at an acute care facility in San Antonio, Texas where she has lived for the past 25 years.

Her list of certifications include: CCS (certified coding specialist); CDIP (certified documentation improvement practitioner) and CCDS (certified clinical documentation specialist). She has a Bachelor of Science degree in Nuclear Medicine Science from Incarnate Word College (now University of the Incarnate Word) and is a veteran of the United States Air Force. She is the mother and grandmother of one son and one grandson.

Chapter 12

Creating Your Own Elegance

I learned about elegance when I was in the third grade. I wanted my mother to buy me elegance for Easter. Even though it was a very long time ago, I vividly recall the day my third-grade teacher, Ms. Jones, wrote the word elegance on the chalkboard. And, next to the word, she defined it for the class. She said the word meant graceful or beautiful, then she instructed the class to use the word in a sentence. As soon as I finished writing my sentence, I raised my hand to be called on. Ms. Jones immediately acknowledged my hand, and I read my sentence. I had written, "I would like my mother to buy me elegance for Easter so that I can look more beautiful than everyone in my family," or something like that.

> *"Elegance is not something you buy. It is something you are."*

I was so proud of my sentence. My teacher chuckled a little after I read my sentence, then she looked at me and said, "Elegance is not something you buy. It is something you are." Some of my classmates laughed at me because I had not used the term correctly. I felt like I had disappointed my teacher and was embarrassed, but I did not get upset. I just smiled and laid my head on my desk. Ms. Jones saw what happened and said, "You just demonstrated a form of elegance." I didn't think I had done anything special. I just smiled and put my head on my desk. I was a little confused by her statement because I had no idea what I had done. My teacher said, "You demonstrated elegance in the way you reacted to your classmates." How had I demonstrated elegance? What did I do that was elegant? Did I create my own elegance in third grade?

As I reflect on that memory, I realize that day started my journey of creating my own sense of elegance. I am not certain that I demonstrated elegance, but my teacher sure made me feel like I was an elegant student. She taught me a valuable lesson that day that I never forgot. She taught me that you create your own sense of elegance by the way you act, treat other people, carry yourself and react to adversity. She taught me that elegance is a state of being, not necessarily something you buy in the store. I use the term 'necessarily' because you can buy elegant objects that give you a sense of elegance. Material objects can certainly make you feel elegant.

For me, creating my own elegance is a state of being, complimented with style. I truly believe my third-grade teacher was correct when she said that elegance is not something you can buy, it is something you are. But I would be dishonest if I said I did not feel a sense of elegance when I put on a new fitted red dress with studded buttons on the sleeves, black high heeled pointed toe pumps and large diamond studded earrings. I would not be telling the truth if I said getting my nails done with a beautiful coat of platinum gel polish on them did not make me feel a sense of elegance. Furthermore, I would be lying if I said I did not feel a sense of elegance when my hair was natural, neat and styled in two strand twists or Afro puffs.

> To create my own elegance, I smile at people and greet them with kindness.

The forms of elegance described above demonstrate the outward shell of elegance. For me to create my own elegance, my outward appearance must compliment my inner being. Styled elegantly in my red dress, black pumps, diamond studs, polished nails and naturally neat hair, I better be treating people with respect and admiration. To create my own elegance, I smile at people and greet them with kindness. I do not greet them with a superficial smile that you receive from a stranger, but a sincere inviting God freeing smile. A smile that says I see you and respect you. I may not know you, but you are important to me. To create my own elegance, I also talk to people. I engage in meaningful conversations with people. I ask people how they are doing and really want to know how they are doing. Sometimes I will say, "Hi! How are you?" and the person might respond with, "I am fine." I will follow up with, "That is great! I am fine too. I hope you have a wonderful day." When I speak to people in that manner, I feel elegant.

When I am out shopping or running errands with my college aged daughter, she laughs and calls me a "tree hugger" when I greet people in that manner. But I know deep inside she loves the way I interact with people because she always calls me a classy, elegant woman and tells me that she is proud of me. I know I have created a sense of elegance for her and other young people I encounter. I am intentional and specific in the way I demonstrate elegance. I create elegance by my actions, style, class and deeds. I am a proud role model of elegance. I use elegance to help shape the minds, hopes and dreams of every person I meet.

I recall about five years ago, when I became a middle school principal, I loved to walk around the school feeling like God had ordered my steps to serve children. I greeted the students every morning with a smile and a friendly, "Good morning. How are you?" Most of the students greeted me in like manner, most. There was one young lady that refused to smile or say good morning. She just would not. Every morning I spoke to her anyway. One morning I was standing at the door as I always did, and I heard a big ruckus. There was a fight outside, not just any old fight, a girl fight. It was my young lady that refused to speak in the morning against three other girls. I was upset. I took my high heels off, ran down to the side of the building.

> *Creating my own elegance allowed me to help my middle school student find her voice and create a sense of purpose.*

I was extremely angry, but refused to yell, scream or lose my sense of elegance. I softly said to the students with a very stern voice, "There are consequences for your actions and the choices that you make. You will not fight at my school and you will demonstrate self- control." I sent the three high school students with their principal and kept my middle school student with me. I did not say anything further to her for thirty minutes. I had to make sure I demonstrated the behavior that God needed me to demonstrate in that time and space. After an hour had lapsed, I was able to engage in a calm conversation with the student. The conversation was not about the fight. We talked about life and thepurpose of being. She was baffled and confused because I was not upset with her. She did not understand why I was not angry or yelling at her. She began to cry, and I walked over and hugged her. I explained that we all had choices in life, and I chose not to get upset. She did receive consequences for her actions, but she chose not to get upset with me. She chose to create her own elegance, saying she understood and accepted the consequences. I taught the student the same lesson my third-grade teacher taught me, "Elegance is something you are." My student and I had an elegant relationship from that point forward.

Creating my own elegance allowed me to help my middle school student find her voice and create a sense of purpose. Creating my own elegance allowed me to be a role model for my daughter and every person I encounter. Creating my own elegance allowed me to be the God freeing woman I was meant to be. I am elegant because I am fearless. I take risks and challenge the status quo. I created my own sense of purpose through my elegance. How will you create your elegance is the question I ask of thee. Creating my own elegance allows me to be excellent. I will always be the God freeing woman that God created to support people and allow them to support me. Creating my own elegance has allowed me to reach my highest level of being. Creating my own elegance will always make me a proud role model for women, children and my entire community. I am perfect, but creating my own elegance has allowed me to be the best me that is pleasing to God. I will always strive to demonstrate a sense of elegance and gracefulness in everything I do.

How will you create your own elegance? Will you put on stylish clothes? Will you get your hair done, put makeup on and high heels? Will your elegance be created through your actions and deeds? Will you treat people like you want to be treated to feel a sense of elegance? Will you smile and greet each person you meet? Does your elegance need to be revamped, revised, modified or will you be starting from scratch? Whether you are elegant now or plan to become elegant later, you can demonstrate the sense of elegance that

God wants you to demonstrate. Let's all create our elegance together!

Dr. Jimmie Bullard has over 20 years' experience in the field of urban education. She has a strong background in educating the urban learner, including extensive experiences as an African Centered teacher, assistant principal and principal. She loves working with diverse populations of students in the urban core of Kansas City, Missouri. As a matter of fact, she is a proud product of Kansas City Public Schools. She currently is serving as the principal for Longfellow Elementary School in the KCPS district.

Dr. Bullard received her Bachelor's degree in Elementary Education and her first Masters of Education degree in the field of Guidance and Counseling from Lincoln University. She then completed her second Master's Degree in School Administration from William Woods University.

She completed her Doctorate in Urban Leadership and Administration through the University of Missouri Kansas City.

Dr. Bullard has published several poems, articles and is in the process of completing a book in effective classroom management strategies for the urban teacher and a children's book series. She is a member of the Urban Education Leadership Initiative, the Lincoln University Alumni Association, Delta Sigma Theta Sorority and numerous other professional organizations.

Dr. Bullard enjoys writing children's books and poetry, reading, physical fitness and watching professional football, especially the Kansas City Chiefs. Dr. Bullard and her husband reside in the Kansas City area with their two children and dog.

Chapter 13

Reroute

Life was good. In fact, it was great. I had been in Southern California for about two years shortly after graduating college. I was quickly moving up the corporate ladder and living the life of a bachelor. In addition to my full-time job, I worked with my fraternity in community service efforts and worked part-time at a local Boys & Girls Club (BGC). I even played semi-pro football for a short period of time. I was rarely at home, but my busyness was cherished.

I went to church probably more than most men in their early 20s, but that's not saying much. It was seemingly only when convenient and mostly out of guilt in case a loved one asked, "How was church today?" Prayers were consistent, but my effort behind them wasn't. Things would soon turn sour but it was a slow, grinding process.

In early 2008, the Great Recession was just a few months old, and I was in a bit of denial of its potential devastation. I had just lost my job due to downsizing and was now scrapping for extra hours at the BGC. I would watch the news, see people in long unemployment lines and think to myself, I have a bachelor's degree, so I'll be fine.

> As a prideful man, I stressed myself out with the thought of calling my parents and asking for help.

I was eventually promoted to a Site Director role at the BGC, but that's when things got worse. My now full-time employer relied on state funding and with the current state of the economy, our staff went several weeks without payment. Management wrote us a letter about what was happening and gave us $100 cash to help tide us over after weeks of missed and bounced paychecks. This is not at all a reflection on the BGC. It was just the current state of affairs in that region. To add fuel to the fire, gas prices skyrocketed so every move I made was literally calculated. I was financially responsible for the most part. I normally only spent money on flying home to Kansas City, MO, for the holidays so this was very frustrating.

Home is ultimately what I had to lean on. As a prideful man, I stressed myself out with the thought of calling my parents and asking for help. I've failed at that point. That was my last resort, and I did everything I could to avoid it. The little bit of savings I had went to paying my car note, student loans and rent, but that was now depleted. I sold just about everything I owned of value to a local pawn shop and even claimed exempt so I could get every penny of my paycheck. I thought I was at rock bottom.

Every day for the next eight months, I spent my time applying for jobs from 5am until around 1pm before I had to go to work. No one was really hiring so I eventually applied to a rental car company. A place I said I would never work, but ultimately knew I'd get the job. The only opening was, ironically, in Dallas where my girlfriend – ex at the time – lived. I figured we'd get back together and no longer have to deal with the pressure of a long distance relationship. I accepted the job with a drastic cut in pay, but it was a job nonetheless.

I was very depressed. To make matters worse, my new job kept pushing back my start date.

I needed extra money for moving costs and finally made the call to my parents. They sent what they could. I remember crying to my mother over the phone and she comforted me with her words as if I was seven years old learning of my parents' divorce. Other friends, family, even co-workers who knew my challenges helped me out. It was a sobering moment to say the least.

It was November 2008 and the presidential election was taking place just days before I moved to Texas. I was able to help count paper ballots overnight for a $150 paycheck. I figured that would help when I got to Texas as I had enough money to get me there and rent wouldn't be due for another thirty days or so.

The election served as a very uplifting moment, and I was able to take my mind off my reality for a few hours. Things were looking up.

I arrived in Dallas and unpacked what I was able to bring with me. I had no furniture, no bed and no television. Just two laptops – one I was able to keep from the BGC, and the other was one I purchased while I was employed. I figured I had sold everything else I owned, I would at least keep these, so I could continue to look for a better job.

My girlfriend and I fought more than anything, so we stopped seeing each other. This time, I felt it was for good. Another two years passed before we saw each other again. I was very depressed. To make matters worse, my new job kept pushing back my start date. Another month went by and I was without a paycheck. I resorted to selling beats I made on my laptop and allowed the apartment complex manager to talk me into getting a payday loan to pay the rent. It was the worst idea ever, but these are the things you do when you have nowhere else to turn.

I felt anxiety crawling up my back as I was running out of options, and bills continued to pile up. 2009 came and I was finally getting paid, but there was nothing left over for me. I was paying back a loan with an extremely high interest rate. The IRS was garnishing my paycheck for claiming exempt the year before, and my car was repossessed. I also failed to pay my last electric bill in California so that was on my credit along with everything else. Right when I got paid I'd withdraw about $20-$40 so I at least had something to use for the next two weeks. That way I didn't lose it to the looming overdraft fees that were certain to happen. The struggle was most definitely real.

I didn't know anyone in Dallas really. I mostly hung out with people from my job because we all worked the same shift, and it was late in the evening when we got off. I wasn't going to church because I normally worked on Sundays. I was even thinking about selling drugs just to get by. Some of the people I sold beats to did, and it crossed my mind more times than I could count. I didn't want to sink that low but what else could I do? That's when other thoughts seeped into my head that I'm not proud of.

My lowest point was when my lights got cut off during a very cold winter/spring season. I was able to scrounge enough money together to buy an inflatable bed but with the power off it was losing air and the unevenness caused me a lot of pain in my back. The lights were off for almost two months. I slept curled up on my closet floor because my body heat made it bearable. I would go to the small apartment complex gym in the middle of the night to use my electric shaver in the mirror. I'd get home from work and soak Ramen noodles in cold water to eat. I'd even steal a bunch of the fruit and granola bars that were left for customers in the lobby at my job, so I'd have something to eat on my off days. Then, I got a call from my apartment complex. I thought someone reported me shaving in the gym. Instead, they told me someone had broken into my apartment. I was devastated.

> *I didn't have a church home, but I had my Bible. I would sit on my floor against the wall, flip my Bible open and let it fall to a random page.*

I rushed home, and the first thing the police told me was that my power was out. He mistakenly thought the thieves were somehow responsible for that. I just ignored him to save myself the embarrassment of telling the truth. Thankfully, I had one laptop with me as I made music on my lunch breaks. However, the burglars were able to get their hands on the other laptop, several clothing items, shoes and some old DVDs. What hurt most is that they stole my conference championship rings from my days of playing college football. After everyone left, I sat in the middle of my living room floor and cried out to God, asking Him why was this happening to me. Who steals from someone who literally has nothing? Feeling no one cared about me – not my ex, not my family or friends – I felt like ending it all. Things got really dark for me as I fell into a deep depression and pondered suicide. Thankfully, after a few weeks, I started to deepen my relationship with God – in my own way.

I didn't have a church home, but I had my Bible. I would sit on my floor against the wall, flip my Bible open and let it fall to a random page. I'd read it and make it relate to me as best I could. Most of the time, I couldn't make sense of it all, but it helped me.

Stories like Job's let me know it could be much worse, but for my story to be told I'd have to be here to tell it. There were some other bumps in the road for me for sure – toxic relationships, struggling to find myself, more financial woes, etc. But I knew that all-in- all I had to be HERE. It's where I was meant to be.

I put my pain into making music and other forms of artwork – drawing, photography and writing. I took myself out of relationships and situations that weren't the best for me. It was at this time that I was able to reconnect with the woman I can undoubtedly call my first love. We had both just gotten out of a bad relationship so it seemed like perfect timing.

Things were getting better, and I joined my girlfriend's church. It seemed like every Sunday the choir would sing a song that gave me goosebumps and put tears in my eyes. I felt something was changing in me. Not only was it spiritual, it was emotional and mental. I prayed for knowledge and guidance to take me away from where I was, not for a better job or more money but just to get as far away from the recent past as I could. I couldn't be the man I was meant to be if I stayed on that path. I was rerouted. My girlfriend and I dated for three years while I worked hard on getting my finances right and learning this new me. I proposed in 2012, and we wed in 2013. I started a few small side jobs to bring in additional streams of income and used that same passion with art that helped keep me sane. We welcomed a baby boy in 2015, and my relationship with God has never been stronger, due in part to the new church my wife and I joined together.

I could easily say some cliché line here to close this out, but I won't. All I know is that after reading all of this, if you don't think there is a God, if you don't think that He can bring you out of your darkest times, then you are highly mistaken and foolish. Those losses were lessons – not only for me but for others.

Be optimistic, stay blessed and prayers up!

Darrell Robinson, Jr. was born in Springfield, MO and was raised in both Kansas City, MO and Olathe, KS. He wed his lovely wife Brittany in 2013 and they welcomed their son Jaden in 2015. They live in Dallas, TX.

"D.J." graduated from MidAmerica Nazarene University with a Bachelor's in Mass Communications on a Track and Football scholarship. He spends his time with family and running his small businesses such as Antone Productions (music production), AP Beats + Tees (t-shirt design and printing) and Darrell Antone Photography (portraiture). His photography company has seen his work selected for the marketing campaigns of several Fortune 500 companies. He is also the author of the book "The Baby Playbook: A Guide for the Fellas"– a book based on showing men what to expect – and what to do – while their significant other is pregnant.

Darrell is also a proud member of Kappa Alpha Psi Fraternity, Inc. and a member of One Community Church in Plano, TX.

Chapter 14

Finding Yourself

Life is like a game of hide and seek because the only way to win is to find yourself. During this game, you go through times where you're sure that you are headed in the right direction only to realize that you found someone else. When you look in the mirror, you don't recognize the person in front of you. Your smile doesn't look the same, your spirit is low and now you are fueled with negativity. You have successfully taken on the characteristics of the world, and instead of winning this game, you are accepting the values of your surroundings.

I wouldn't say I questioned God, but I do think my faith took a massive hit.

I found myself in this situation not too long ago, but before I get there I want to explain the kind of kid I was growing up. During my early high school years, I was the nerdy but cool guy. I was never really in the in crew, but I was never really out either. I would get invited to some parties, and other times I would be left out. I was kind of on the fence. High school can be rough on a teenager because you are trying to figure

out your place in the world without the context of life. At that age, I was not woke enough to realize that it was ok to be different, so I tried to fit in as much as possible whether that be playing football, cursing (it sounds funny, but I never cursed) or trying to sag (I say try because my parents killed that habit real quick).

I was raised with two parents who instilled certain moral values that I held on to even at that young age. I always had a strong sense of right and wrong. Even when I would do things that were not right, I felt extremely bad about it. I like to believe my conscious is what has kept me on the straight and narrow. I was also the kid who was in church every Sunday, so I think that is why I tended to stay out of trouble. Halfway through my high school years, tragedy struck my family. My dad was killed in car accident during my sophomore year. This was a very tough time, especially for a fifteen-year-old boy. I was heartbroken, confused and angry. I wouldn't say I questioned God, but I do think my faith took a massive hit. I had a strong tie to God, but after the accident, I felt as if a large piece of my faith left. It wasn't a conscious decision to feel that way; it was more like I didn't recognize the power of God in my life anymore.

In the latter years of high school, there was an altering in my actual being. Looking back, I can tell you that I didn't recognize I had changed, but it was obvious during my college years that I had. During my senior year of high school, I started to feel myself a little bit. When things went well for me, I didn't give the praise to God. I felt as if I was the one who was making the good things happen. I became arrogant and didn't even know it. I wasn't completely removed from my spiritual beliefs. I still attended church on Sundays and I tried to apply the teaching of the Bible to my life, I just didn't own my spirituality. Yes, I claimed I was a Christian, but I wasn't really living a Christian lifestyle. I was going through the motions. Although I was young, I still knew the things you learn and experience effect you later in life. The habits you develop are the hardest to break because you have had time to solidify them as your lifestyle. Compliments were also fueling my ego. I constantly heard from family

> *I quickly realized that I was attending school with people who may be having their first interaction with a black person ever.*

members that they were proud of me. My peers often told me they were curious about how I pushed through such tragedy. I never answered that question with a humbling response. It was more of a, "I don't know how I did it, I just did." I thought perhaps I was just different from everyone. I really thought I had some superior way of dealing with high stress levels. I would soon realize anything I was able to do was not because of my doing.

That game of hide and seek I mentioned earlier is very tricky because you don't realize you are actually playing. During those younger years, you think every encounter, experience, and decision you make is minor. You don't realize your choices are molding you into a perfectly imperfect human. At the end of my high school career, I had found a young man who was damaged, naïve, and arrogant. I was becoming a new individual and I couldn't see the clues.

The beginning of my freshmen year of college was exciting. It was a fresh start, and I would be on my own for the first time, making all my own decisions. I would have my own spot (although I wouldn't call a dorm room a spot). I would be in control of my life or at least I thought. As the semester kicked off, I found myself trying to get acclimated with the culture shock of being around various people with different beliefs. I quickly realized that I was attending school with people who may be having their first interaction with a black person ever. That definitely affected the way I maneuvered through college. I got involved on campus, going to different groups, activities and seminars. I figured that would be the best way for me to learn about how to deal with these new circumstances. I learned about code switching, implicit bias, and different communication theories. With this new knowledge, there was nothing anyone could tell me. I was officially a know it all. Although I gained new information, I was lacking in my spiritual intellect.

As I continued to fill myself with new knowledge, I also started a new habit. I became a casual drinker. Although this is a common activity that takes place in college, it wasn't something I was ever interested in. Before college, I never drank. My first experience with alcohol was unexplainable. All I know is all my inhibitions were lowered, and I was able to become this super outgoing person that I never was. I was the life of the party, and the attention I received went straight to my head. As my college career continued, I went out on Tuesdays, Thursdays, Fridays and Saturdays. People I had never met around campus recognized me. They would say things like, "Hey,

I know you had a great night" or "You ready to turn up again?" At first, I thought it was cool that people knew me, but as it continued to happen, I became embarrassed about it. Once my roommate started hearing about my nights from his teammates, I knew I needed to settle down. My roommate called me the mayor of Pittsburgh because I was out so much. It's not like this experience was exclusive to me, I also heard stories about everyone else, which made it easier for me to justify my behavior. I was slowly turning into a follower.

During my latter college years, the partying and drinking amped up, and to make it worse, I became the DJ at most parties. I had a reputation as one of the best DJ's on campus. The compliments came back, and I ate them up. I was so full of myself, I bragged about how I had the whole city popping. At the time, I thought it was marketing, but looking back, I was just looking for more positive affirmation. Being in environments where heavy drinking was part of my job made it ten times harder to relax. It got to

> *Once I graduated, real life hit me. I was happy, nervous and scared at the same time. I had no clue what I was about to do.*

the point where I was living just to get to the weekend. Although my behavior didn't affect my grades tremendously, it did inhibit me from being the best student I could be. On days when I knew I had a test, I skipped studying to be out with friends. I was doing things backwards. I became a man I never thought I would become. I was getting all my value from the wrong things. I was lost, and I didn't know it, and this would continue after graduation.

Once I graduated, real life hit me. I was happy, nervous and scared at the same time. I had no clue what I was about to do. I didn't have any job offers lined up. I'm sure this could be attributed to my lack of preparation. My GPA wasn't where it could have been. I didn't have money, so that meant I was going back home with my mom and stepdad. This meant all the habits I picked up in college would have to be hidden because I knew I couldn't continue to act like that in my mama's house. After six months of job searching, I finally landed two jobs. I got my first big boy job and I had a serving job on the side. I was so excited because the money was about to start rolling in and it did. I had never seen that much money before as a twenty-two year old man. Guess what that meant? "PARTY!" I went back to my old ways, except now I had a little change in my pocket. Once again, I was out on Tuesdays,

Thursday, Fridays, Saturdays and even Sundays. I was living it up. My savings account was looking good and my wardrobe was upgraded. Once again there was nothing you could tell me because I was the man. The compliments came in, and I was able to help other people out. I was successful. What I didn't know was that I was going to be humbled real soon.

Being back home was an adjustment. My mom was in my ear telling me to be careful when I went somewhere. Even if I was making a quick trip around the corner, she said, "Be careful." It annoyed me because I was grown. I knew what I was supposed to do. My arrogant attitude began to show; the tone of my voice reflected my irritation. I was completely out of line, but life had something in store for me to check my ego.

One Saturday after work, I received a call from a friend telling me we are about to go out. That was nothing new. I went home to get ready then went over to my friend's house. We were having a great time conversing, dancing and drinking. I heard someone say, "SHOT TIME." That was our phrase when it was time to drink, and I readied my glass. We had several rounds, but I'm not sure how many. By the time I hopped in my friend's car and we headed to the bar, I was in a good place. We had more drinks, and this continued for some time. By the end of the night, I was not sober, but I wasn't sloppy drunk. It was apparent though that I needed to chill. We made it back to my friend's house where I would normally crash to avoid drinking and driving, but for some reason that night I thought I could make it home. I told my friends I was headed home, and they said, "HELLL NAHH, you are too drunk to be driving. You are staying here!" They convinced me to stay, but once everyone went to sleep, I got up and left. That was the worst decision I made in my life. All the arrogance, compliments and knowledge culminated into that one decision.

That morning, I awaken to some taps on my window. "Hello, are you alright? Sir, are you alright?" I rolled down the window to a man asking me what happened. I looked around and my car was in a ditch facing a lake. I immediately started to panic because I had no clue how I got there. I told the man I was alright, but he insisted that he could help. Thinking I could do everything on my own, I kept telling him I would figure it out. He said, "ok" and left. I tried to push my car. I called my friends, but they were still asleep. I didn't want to call my mom or stepdad because I didn't want them to panic. It got to the point where I just got in my car and put my head on the steering wheel. "Tap! Tap! Tap." I lifted my head from the wheel and the same man was there again. He asked me if

I wanted a ride to the gas station, and I said yes. At that point, I didn't realize he was my blessing, but he was. He dropped me off at the gas station and I called for a tow truck. I thought I would tell my parents I got into an accident and avoid telling them the truth. Boy was I wrong. When the tow truck driver picked me up and took me to my car, two officers and my stepdad were there. The relief on my stepdad's face told it all: an empty car that he has positively identified as his son's car by a lake.

Luckily, my mom was out of town, so she didn't have to wake up to a doorbell with two officers saying we found your son's car, but he is not in it. The officers asked me if alcohol or drugs were the cause of this. I said no; I was not about to snitch on myself. But I could tell they knew based on the location that it was a little more than speeding going on. They scolded me for a few minutes then let me go. After the incident, I went home and cried. I had embarrassed myself and let my family down. Never in a million years would they have thought I would be drinking and driving. I could have killed myself or worse, killed someone else because of my stupidity. I was upset with myself because I thought I was invincible. That day I became a weak, foolish and naïve man. I hit rock bottom, and I knew I had to do some real soul searching in order to fix myself. To this day, I still don't think I have properly thanked God for watching over me in that situation. I don't know how I could thank Him for that amount of grace because most people don't get second chances. I would have lost the game of hide and seek and lived eternally with a person I was never intended to be.

As humans we are constantly in a battle with ourselves. That day God gave me a second chance to find myself. He allowed me to keep looking, in hopes that one day I would find out who I'm really supposed to be. He humbled me, and He showed me that as much stuff as I think I have, it can all be taken away in a second. In my life, I have been blessed with so many chances that I'm not even deserving. But it would be a spit in the face of the Lord to not strive to get better with every chance. I would like to say that at the end of that I became an enlightened individual, but that was not the case. Every day is a struggle to learn a little bit more about myself, to be more empathetic, to be more appreciative and to just be a better person. I realize the game of hide and seek takes a lifetime because you will constantly grow and regress. At the end of the day, all you can do is thank the Lord for the time you get to play.

Darrell Chism was born and raised in Kansas City, MO. He is a young music producer/writer  and is the co-founder of Lighthouse Music. He began making music at 16 and has already performed at some of the best venues in Kansas City and is respected as strong up-and- coming talent. His latest album, "For the Moment" proves to continue his recent success. Darrell graduated from Pittsburg State University where he received his Bachelor's degree in Management and Marketing. Darrell wants to share how he lost connection with God, but has found his way back and strengthened his relationship. This will be his first published piece of writing. He is looking forward to sharing his story with you.

Concluding Thought

From Rochinda Pickens

How do you feel after reading the truth of each story? Which chapters resonated with you the most? And how can you use their experiences to help you move forward in your own life? I can only imagine how you are feeling, you can't believe someone else is telling your story. Did you notice the common denominator we each shared?

Yes, an undeniable father who has kept each of us through it all. I'm so grateful that you decided that beyond the fear freedom does exist, and the only way to be freed from the past you must move forward by taking that first step. That first step will feel uncomfortable in the beginning but the realization of mobility will set in quickly. The silent affliction that kept you paralyzed for years has finally been unleashed. The divine instructions from God intentionally inserted in your soul years ago have finally showed up in your next assignment called "LIFE". As you look at your masterpiece completely transformed from the broken, shattered glass you finally have the answer you have been seeking. Do you remember when you were lovestruck by that unknown prospect that caught you off guard? It helped you tell your story until it was heard loud and clear. No longer will you be caught off guard, you have been summoned and served by God to start over.

Now pull out that calendar and start dating with a purpose, a purpose that has revealed to all there is life after death. As you create your own elegance while on this journey we call reroute through life sit quietly and thank God for allowing you to pick up the pieces and find yourself.

Your new beginning starts NOW!

Blessings,

Rochinda

Rochinda Pickens

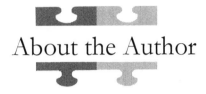

About the Author

Rochinda Pickens is a vessel being used by God, a loving wife, author, speaker, grandma and proud mother of three. She is a connector to women globally and has a heart for all. Rochinda's courage and determination to walk in "Freedom" has impacted and inspired women to stand in their authentic being. As founder and Chief Executive Officer of Kept Woman of God, Inc 501(c)(3) nonprofit organization, she has helped many define their own truth and is making a difference in surrounding communities throughout the United States. Rochinda, has helped develop workshops, retreats and annual conferences that have transformed the lives of women. Rochinda is the author of *From Being Kept to Being Kept*, a journey about freedom and elevation through God's surrender. Born and raised in Kansas City, Missouri an avid philanthropist and a helper to those in need. She is a member of Sister Circle of Greater Kansas City. She travels the world speaking and sharing her signature message "Walking In Freedom."

Learn more about Rochinda Pickens online at www.KeptWomanofGod.com

 @keptwoman0711

 @keptwomanofGod

 @keptwomanofGod

 @keptwoman0711

KEPT WOMAN OF GOD
CONFERENCE

VOLUNTEER. EXHIBIT. SPONSOR.

While women have been given countless opportunities to connect virtually with other women from all over the world, it never quite takes the place of connecting in person-hugging the necks of sisters in Christ and sitting down to conversation over coffee.

This event is more than just a meet-and-greet - it's an immersion in the kind of love and encouragement that comes from women connecting in real life.

Join the Kept Woman of God Ministry to support women in our community.

SPEAKER.   AUTHOR.   COACH.

ROCHINDA PICKENS
"AND YOU WILL KNOW THE TRUTH AND THE TRUTH WILL MAKE YOU FREE." -JOHN 8:32

http://www.KeptWomanofGod.com

ROCHINDA
PICKENS

KEPT WOMAN OF GOD MINISTRY
http://www.KeptWomanofGod.com

FREEDOM

NEED A COACH?
Hire
**ROCHINDA
PICKENS**

For You formed my inward parts;
You covered me in my mother's womb.
Psalm 139:13.
New King James Version (NKJV)

http://www.KeptWomanOfGod.com

Made in the USA
Lexington, KY
08 March 2018